THE IRISH
WISE GUYS

D1637639

THE IRISH WISE GUYS

The Stories of the Most Notorious Irish-American Gangsters

JOHN JOE McGINLEY

Ballpoint Press

Published in 2020 by Ballpoint Press
4 Wyndham Park, Bray,
Co Wicklow, Republic of Ireland.

Telephone: 00353 86 821 7631
Email: ballpointpress1@gmail.com
Web: www.ballpointpress.ie

ISBN 978-1-9160863-5-7

While every effort has been made to ensure the accuracy
of all information contained in this book, neither the author nor
the publisher accepts liability for any errors or omissions made.

Book design and production by Joe Coyle Media&Design,
joecoyledesign@gmail.com

Back page photograph: The funeral of Vincent 'Mad Dog' Coll

Printed and bound by GraphyCems

Contents

Acknowledgements

THEY say everyone has a book in them. I hope I have more than one and what a place to start than with the tale of 17 men who ruled the American underworld throughout the 19th and 20th centuries.

I would like to thank my wife Eileen who encouraged me when I doubted I could do this and who spent hours correcting my spelling and editing this book for me. I could never have done this without her support and I dedicate this book to her and her patience.

Special thanks has to go to Joe Coyle who designed my front cover and I appreciate the time he spent creating a wonderful image to support the tales I have to tell.

I would like to thank Joe McCormack who gave me invaluable help in making my ideas a reality.

Finally I would like to acknowledge the men who I have chosen to write about — the Irish Wise Guys themselves. A group of individuals whose lives were so similar and whose destinies in many cases became linked.

Violence was their profession and crime their calling, but I can't help but think that in different circumstances, away from the poverty and hardship they faced, that perhaps they could have been different men. We shall never know, but this book is at least their story and I hope you enjoy it.

Introduction
The Irish in America

THE United States has always opened its arms to the huddled masses of Irish men and women, who have left their native land for a better life, and most have repaid this hospitality many times over.

Twenty-two of the 45 presidents of the United States claim Irish descent. The first man on the moon Neil Armstrong's ancestors came from Fermanagh and Tyrone. In the world of business, Henry Ford, the inventor of the modern assembly line, considered himself both an American and a West Cork man.

When you think of the Irish in America, an iconic image is of the cops who pounded the beat of New York and other major American cities such as Boston and Chicago.

However, an unsavoury side to the Irish in America has always been the rise of — and violence caused by — the Irish gangsters. This book will highlight the stories of the most famous of these men, many of whom became America's most wanted criminals and some even Public Enemy Number 1.

By the American War of Independence in 1775, 250,000 Irishmen and women had emigrated to America. The first wave of Irish had begun with Ulster plantation Protestants leaving the northern counties to escape English trade restrictions and in search of greater religious freedom and prosperity across the Atlantic.

While the stereotype of Irish emigrants is often of poor peasants fleeing famine, this was not the case for the first wave of Irish, many of whom prospered. One such Ulsterman was Charles Carroll who emigrated during colonial times. His grandson, also Charles Carroll, was one of the signatories of the Declaration of Independence.

As the industrial revolution transformed America, the early Irish settlers abandoned the farms they had established and migrated once again towards the cities in search of factory work.

Cities such as Boston, Philadelphia and Chicago grew rapidly as did their Irish population.

As the cities expanded the demand for infrastructure and transport networks grew with them as did the job opportunities for Irish men and women.

The Irish who came to America in the early 1820s and 30s found ample but arduous opportunities in factories, building canals and railways. Soon Irish enclaves were being formed all over America but the largest populations were centred along the eastern seaboard in New York, New England, New Jersey and Pennsylvania.

Between 1820 and 1860, the Irish constituted over one third of all immigrants to the United States.

These Irish immigrants, driven by An Gort Mhor ('the great hunger'), were different to the earlier immigrants. These were not Protestants looking for new opportunities, who assimilated almost seamlessly into American life, but the Catholic Irish driven from their homeland by hunger and who were just looking to survive.

They were by and large poor, unskilled and unfamiliar to urban life; worse still, they were Roman Catholic. In the growing America these Irishmen and women with a perceived allegiance to Rome were not welcome.

The Irish of the Famine era were willing to work for very little pay and this, along with their religion, stoked animosity. The cancer of sectarian conflict that had blighted Ireland for centuries found its way to the new world and soon led to violence. St Mary's Catholic Church was burned down in New York City and in 1844 riots in Philadelphia left many dead.

Soon political groups sprang up to capitalise on this wave of anti-Irish and anti-Catholic sentiment. One such group made famous in the film *Gangs of New York* was the American political party known as the nativist 'Know Nothings'. They obtained this nickname due to their standard reply to any question regarding their rule's regulations and attacks on the Irish immigrants, which was:

"I know nothing about that."

Their central tenet was to fight against foreign influences and:

"...elect to all offices of Honour, Profit, or Trust, no one but native-born citizens of America, of this Country to the exclusion of all Foreigners, and to all Roman Catholics, whether they be of native or Foreign Birth, regardless of all-party predilections whatever."

This creed helped ensure the election of many anti-Irish politicians, making life even harder for the newly arrived Irish.

However, by the late 19th and early 20th centuries the Irish immigrants and their children had begun to rise from poverty and despair, using attributes such as unity, their escalating numbers and their right to vote. The Irish would find salvation and power in politics.

The Irish in numbers organised to ensure the rise of political leaders who would fight for them when elected. Labour unions sprung up and were soon dominated by Irishmen who ensured decent paying jobs for themselves and other Irish immigrants.

Throughout America and especially in the east coast Irish social clubs became the refuge and rescue of many in this new strange land.

The Roman Catholic Church, long despised by the American establishment, grew rapidly to become a major force in American life with its Irish wing championing Irish values.

New York, America's most powerful city and a cultural melting pot, was the main focus of Irish transformation and influence. New York Harbour was the modern Plymouth Rock for the Irish. Around 75pc of the Famine Irish landed in New York Harbor, and by 1860 a quarter of New York City's population was Irish.

The Irish soon controlled Tammany Hall, the Democratic Party political machine which held an iron and corrupt grip on much of New York politics. The rise of the Irish political machine in New York was complete when Al Smith, the grandson of Irish immigrants, was elected Governor of New York State in 1918.

The rise of the union movement also provided opportunities for Irish immigrants and many Irish helped establish and run unions throughout America, some of which would be highly influential such as the International Longshoreman's Union.

By the end of the 19th century, the Irish had fully permeated every aspect of American culture.

As the young America began to mature between the wars the Irish established themselves in all walks of life — including crime — and I would like to share with you now the tales of the most famous and influential Irish American gangsters and their gangs who ruled the streets of New York, Boston and Chicago. These men are the Irish Wise Guys.

The extreme poverty in Hell's Kitchen gave rise to the birth of street gangs, organised crime syndicates during Prohibition and the evolution of many who would go down in gangster folklore

1

The Gophers

THE environment in which you are born and reared can have a dramatic impact on your personality and life chances. The men who became the most notorious Irish-American gangsters were no different. They had the intelligence and determination to have become model and successful citizens if they had been born in different circumstances. It was this very intelligence and drive that allowed them to drag themselves out of the poverty they experienced and to reach what they perceived as success, albeit for a very short time in many instances.

Loners like Vincent 'Mad Dog' Coll are rare in the annals of Irish-American gangsters who mostly achieved notoriety as part of the many gangs that sprung up almost from the first moments Irish immigrants came off the Famine boats in New York or settled in Boston and Chicago. Gangs like The Gophers, The White Hand Gang, The Northside Gang, The Winter Hill Gang and The Westies.

No story of Irish-American gangsters would be complete without a look at each of these gangs, who were the stepping stone for so many in their rise up the world of crime.

The Gophers

The Gophers were acknowledged as the undisputed kings of crime in Hell's Kitchen for many years. Their domain ran from Seventh Avenue to Eleventh Avenue and from Fourteenth Street to Forty-Second Street.

Hell's Kitchen had a reputation for poverty and crime which was endemic given its proximity to the Hudson River docks, where the first German and Irish immigrants found work and eventually formed gangs in the 19th century.

Geographically Hell's Kitchen was an area in Mid-Manhattan, running from 34th street to 57th Street, west of Eighth Avenue running down to the Hudson River.

The first settlers — mostly Irish and free African-Americans — lived in a network of shambolic and filthy shanty towns, where crime, sex and violence were an everyday occurrence and for many, an occupation.

With gangs such as the Hell's Kitchen Gang, The Gorillas, The Parlour Mob, and The Gophers, the neighbourhood soon became known for its violence.

There are numerous stories of how the area got its name.

The first time the name was mentioned in print was on the September 22, 1881. A *New York Times* reporter covering a story on a particularly gruesome multiple murder referred to an infamous tenement at 39th Street and 10th Avenue as being in:

> 'Hell's kitchen' and that the area was 'probably the lowest and filthiest in the city'.

Another story goes that a veteran New York police man was sagely watching a riot between rival gangs on west 39th Street near 10th Avenue with a young partner. The rookie, appalled by the carnage, turned and said:

'This place is hell itself'.

The cop, who went by the name of Dutch Fred, calmly responded:

"Hell's a mild climate. This is Hell's Kitchen."

The extreme poverty in the area gave rise to the birth of street gangs, organised crime syndicates during Prohibition and the evolution of many who would go down in gangster folklore.

The area witnessed four distinct waves of immigration — the first was escaped slaves from the south; then free African-Americans who worked on the Croton Aqueduct in the 1840s; third came the German settlers who soon moved on to the more agriculturally suitable mid-west; and finally came the coffin ships from the Irish Famine. The area soon became an Irish enclave.

This was the case until the 1950s when Puerto Rican immigrants arrived in great numbers. Their clashes with their Irish and Italian neighbours inspired Arthur Laurents' *West Side Story*.

It was in Hell's Kitchen that The Gophers got their nickname which came from their fondness for hiding out in the maze-like basements and cellars of the slum tenements of old New York. The main area of criminal activity of The Gophers was the New York Central railroad yards which ran through their territory up to the far west side.

The Gopher Gang evolved from various local street gangs in the 1890s, into what later became a committee which met semi-regularly at their headquarters known as Battle Row, a saloon owned by a minor criminal called 'Mallet Murphy'. They met there to plan future criminal activity, sort out feuds and divide profits from their various criminal activities which included robbery, prostitution and numerous gambling dens.

At their peak The Gophers had as many as 500 members. They also had younger apprentice gang members, imaginatively called the 'Baby Gophers'. These young men would eventually evolve into vicious gang members ready to take their place in The Gophers' ranks.

Their power was so strong that they also had client gangs who would pay tribute to them, such as The Parlour Boys, The Gorillas and The Rhodes Gang.

There was a high turnover in the leadership of The Gophers gang. It was rare for a gang leader to last more than a few months. The Gophers did not produce many outstanding leaders. Instead there was a long list of short-lived characters with catchy names like 'Newburgh Gallagher', 'Stumpy' Malarkey, 'One Lung' Curran and 'Goo Goo' Knox, the last of whom helped create another gang, The Hudson Dusters.

However, one man would stand out amongst all the rest in The Gophers — Owney Madden, who we will hear about more in Chapter 12.

An early leader was Malarkey 'One Lung' Curran, who during his tenure as leader had a bizarre claim to fame in his choice of attire, he even started a fashion trend.

Curran was notorious for his brazen attacks on lone police patrolmen. During one such assault he knocked the police officer out and stole his jacket.

He asked his girlfriend to alter it into a 'smart military style' which she did and this helped create a fashion fad.

Over the next few weeks several police officers found themselves beaten up and relieved of their jackets and The Gophers strutted around proudly in their new coats.

The police decided this was a step too far and to avoid future humiliation, they abandoned solo patrols and began entering Gopher territory in groups of four or five ending the short-lived craze and protecting their dignity.

The Gophers even had a female gang, the 'Lady Gophers' or the 'Battle Row Ladies Social and Athletic Club', as they were more formally known. They were led by a Hell's Kitchen legend. Battle Annie, known as the queen of Hell's Kitchen. Many thought she was the most feared brawler of her time.

Born Annie Walsh but forever known as Battle Annie, she was the founder and longtime leader of the gang's female auxiliary, who proved to be as ruthless and vicious as their male counterparts.

When called upon, Battle Annie was able to assemble a fighting force of between 50 and 100 women within hours, all armed with clubs, bricks and knives. These women acted as reserve backup in fights over territorial disputes with other gangs. They often worked as paid strike-breakers by businesses and labour unions throughout a number of violent disputes during the 1870s.

The Lady Gophers did not discriminate. There were few strikes around the early 1900s in New York that Battle Annie didn't provide female muscle for "biting and scratching" either pickets or strike-breakers. It didn't matter to Annie and The Gophers who they attacked as long as they were paid.

Another well-known Gopher was 'Happy Jack' Mulraney. He was called 'Happy Jack' because he always appeared to be smiling. However, he actually suffered from a partial paralysis of the facial muscles. He hated anyone slagging off his facial features and as a well-known psychopath, this was unfortunate for the offenders if they were caught.

Many rival gang members lost their lives for making disparaging remarks about his seemingly benign perpetual grin.

A Hell's Kitchen legend goes that, when a close friend of his, 'Paddy the Priest' once asked 'Happy Jack' why he didn't laugh out the other side of his face, Mulraney responded by shooting him dead.

It is more likely he murdered his friend over a woman or a dispute about money. Whatever the reason for this, 'Happy Jack' was sentenced to life in prison.

In the early 1910s the New York Central Railroad company organised a special police force to stop the pillage and plundering that The Gophers had wreaked upon them. A number of these officers were ex-policemen who had "suffered grievously" at the hands of Gopher gang members. Perhaps some had even lost their coats. They were motivated by a desire to destroy The Gophers and were well paid to do so.

The tide was now ebbing fast away from The Gophers and, subjected to increased police attention and brutality, their power waned. They also lost whatever protection they had from the corrupt Democratic politicians who decided The Gophers were yesterday's men and women with no use for them in modern politics.

Within a few short months The Gophers were a spent force. Their leader Newburgh Gallagher was soon convicted of numerous crimes and sent to Sing Sing prison in Ossining, New York, leaving The Gophers in total disarray.

The gang soon split into three factions with Owney Victor Madden heading the largest group.

Madden was born in Leeds, England in 1891. He was described as "slick, slim and dapper, with the gentle smile of a cherub and the cunning and cruelty of a devil". He arrived in America when he was just a boy and by the time he was seventeen he had already been a suspect in two murders and earned the nickname 'Owney the Killer'. And he slowly began to stabilise what was left of The Gophers gang.

However, in 1914 he fell out with a member of the rival Duster gang 'Little Patsy Doyle', over a woman by the name of Freda Horner. Doyle made the fatal mistake of informing the police about Madden's operations. As a rival suitor, Madden might have beaten him up, but as an informer Madden decided Doyle had to die.

Madden was found guilty of murder and sentenced to 20 years in Sing Sing prison. He was released on bail after nine years and quickly saw the landscape had changed dramatically.

His old gang The Gophers no longer existed, its members were either dead, in jail or had joined other crime gangs growing as a result of Prohibition. Prohibition and organised crime was becoming increasingly sophisticated. The days of the rough and ready street gangs was over, as was the era of The Gophers.

A young Al Capone was sent to Chicago because The White Hand Gang had him on a short list of those that needed to be killed

2

The White Hand Gang

BETWEEN 1900 and 1925 a conflict raged along the New York harbours, a war between Irish and Italian gangs to control the lucrative rackets that were available along the busy and expanding waterfront wharfs and warehouses.

This was the battle between the Italian Sicilian Black Hand Gang and a combination of Irish street gangs who would eventually become known as The White Hand Gang. Their name was chosen in response to the Sicilian Black Hand gangs and carried the implication that the Irish gang was the 'white' counter to the growing presence of what they considered 'non-white' Italian gangsters and Italian immigrants.

Black Hand, of course, was only a description of the methods Italians used, such as kidnapping for ransom, but the many newspapers of the time thought it was an actual gang. In any case, the Irish-Americans in the dock neighbourhood and slums from the Navy Yard all the way down to Red Hook, which were traditionally Irish-held areas since the Potato Famine of the 1840s and 1850s, didn't want the Italians to move up from their strongholds of Bay Ridge, Bensonhurst and Coney Island.

The Irish gangs were famously anti-Italian and not afraid to show it. To maintain their dominance and fight against the encroaching Italian mafia they were extremely violent and members frequently killed each other to achieve leadership positions.

The White Hand Gang evolved from the numerous gangs that populated the Brooklyn waterfront in the late 1800s and early 20th century. One such gang was the Swamp Angels who dominated the dockyards of New York Harbour from the 1850s onwards.

A gang of Irish immigrants, they operated out of Lower Manhattan. Their headquarters gave them access to the newly built sewer network which they utilised to continually raid the East River docks, hijacking ships and stealing cargo which they then sold off within hours before thefts were reported or indeed even discovered.

This ingenious method of criminal activity was countered by the New York Police Department who started placing snipers to guard the waterfront. However, this did not deter the hardy Irish and the robberies continued. The police were forced to take desperate measures and began to send squads down into the sewers to intercept the Swamp Rats. Desperate hand-to-hand battles were not uncommon and the death toll on both sides rose.

Eventually the Swamp Rats abandoned the sewer system as it was just too dangerous but — despite the police snipers — they continued to hijack cargo ships as they were unloaded onto the wharfs.

The authorities began to win the war and by the 1870s

the Swamp Rats were a much diminished force. They had two main Irish rivals — The Red Onion Gang who controlled the Atlantic and Baltic terminals; and The Jay Street Gang who, funnily enough, were based on Jay Street, underneath the Manhattan Bridge.

As the influx of Italian immigrants grew and the Black Hand Sicilian gang structure began to evolve, the Swamp Rats, Red Onion Gang and The Jay Street Gang eventually merged into what would eventually become The White Hang Gang.

The name White Hand Gang first began to be used around 1905 in newspaper reports.

However, they weren't very well organised and, despite large numbers, they were still just a group of out-of-work violent teens. While they had aspirations for greater things, they lacked a leader to harness this ambition. In 1912 a man would step forward, Dinny Meehan.

Dinny Meehan leadership, 1912–1920

Dinny Meehan was originally from the Warren Street Red Onion Gang. Meehan eventually became known as the leader of The White Hand Gang in 1912 when he was 23 years old. His status as leader was cemented when he was exonerated in a sensational trial against him and three of his fellow gang members, for killing one Christie Maroney, a bartender and safe cracker who refused to pay tribute to The White Hand Gang. For this he was shot between the eyes in a Sands Street saloon, where he was working.

At the trial's conclusion when the verdict was to be read, "a large squad of policemen and many detectives and reserves" were summoned as the judge and police felt that if Meehan were to be convicted, a riot would break out at the Kings County Court.

The courtroom was packed with young Irish-American gang members and their girlfriends. Italian Black Hand Gang leaders like Frankie Yale and Johnny Torrio would have been watching from afar as well, hoping Meehan would be convicted.

When the jury decided there wasn't enough proof or reliable witnesses, Meehan was found not guilty and released. The courtroom and the street outside erupted in cheers and Dinny Meehan was made into a legend for bucking and flaunting the system.

From that point forward, The White Hand Gang was ruled with an iron fist and with extraordinary unity, which was so rare for Irish-American gangs of the era.

As WW1 came to an end the White Handers retained a firm grip on the Brooklyn Bridge and Red Hook waterfront. They collected tribute from wharf owners and barge captains. Anyone stupid enough or brave enough to not pay up would see their wharfs and vessels looted; everyone paid.

Each longshoreman had to pay a daily commission for the right to work. This was not as prohibitive a measure as it may seem, many Irishmen were willing to pay the tax as they saw The White Hand Gang as their protectors, ensuring the Italians did not take over the waterfront. It was a price worth paying for job security.

What made The White Hand Gang different from the many street gangs who came before them was due to four factors:

1. In Dinny Meehan, they had a leader who inspired loyalty and who was a genius at organising.

2. They had a very strict code of silence, way more powerful than the Italian Omerta, according to some. They never gave information to the police and kept disputes among themselves to be settled outside of the law, sometimes brutally and ending in death.

3. Because gang members lived in Brooklyn and not Manhattan which many perceived to be Now York City, the police were more lax and left many in the working class community to sort out their own disputes. This created a vacuum The White Hand Gang was happy to fill.

4. Many of The White Hand Gang members originally came from Manhattan. They wanted to leave the now Italian controlled streets behind and continue to live the "old way". This meant many of them already knew how to run a street gang due to their experiences and traditions in old Manhattan, providing readymade criminal expertise and knowledge.

Their power was so fierce and their reputation so all-encompassing in Brooklyn that a young Al Capone was sent to Chicago, as many sources confirm, because The White Hand Gang had him on a short list of those that needed to be killed. The Mafia could not afford to lose one of its rising stars.

In reality, it was one of a few reasons for Capone's moving to Chicago, but it was certainly true that The White Hand Gang was as powerful, if not more powerful, than the Mafia in Brooklyn at the time and Capone was too hot a prospect for the Italians to risk.

Under Meehan, the dock boss at each terminal paid tribute to him at 25 Bridge Street (which was a saloon called The Dock Loaders' Club, though the gang's headquarters was right above it).

Every labourer that was used to unload or load a ship or truck or freight rail had to first report to Dinny Meehan under the Manhattan Bridge. If a factory or warehouse in the neighbourhood (like the Empire Stores warehousing units) refused to pay tribute, Meehan and his boys would steal from it. If a ship captain didn't pay tribute, people like 'Cinders' Connolly, one of Meehan's men, would set it ablaze and loosen its ties to the pier bollards, letting it burn in the East River.

If a gang member talked too much, he'd be found in his bed with a gunshot to his face or with his hands tied behind his back in the New York Harbour.

The gang was also hired as 'starkers', a term that is outdated today, which meant that, for example, the International Longshoremen's Association (ILA) might hire The White Hand Gang to kill or maim a New York Dock Company employee who refused to pay their union dues. Or, by contrast, the New York Dock Company might hire the gang to kill a particularly obnoxious ILA man.

In any case, with Meehan as the leader, things were organised. Everyone knew who to go to when they needed a job or needed someone killed or maimed. Everyone knew what the rules were and the penalty for breaking them.

A prominent gang member, 'Wild' Bill Lovett was five years younger than Dinny Meehan, and at the beginning of Prohibition in 1920, he started spreading ideas about getting in on the up-and-coming bootlegging and illegal distillery boom (an Irishtown tradition).

He was a talented gangster with a wild temper when drunk, but very intelligent sober. On top of that, he was a decorated veteran of the First World War, something that gave him a powerful status of his own among the longshoremen gangsters, labourers and factory workers along the Brooklyn waterfront.

Suddenly, The White Hand Gang that had enjoyed so much success and underground notoriety under Dinny Meehan from 1912 to the early 1920 had two leaders — a recipe for trouble.

In the afternoon of March 31, 1920, Dinny Meehan was shot multiple times while in bed with his wife Sadie (who was wounded in the shoulder). No one was charged for Meehan's murder, but everyone knew it was Wild Bill Lovett that either carried it out, or ordered the murder. The White Hand Gang now had only one leader.

'Wild' Bill Lovett leadership, 1920–1923

Bill Lovett was a decorated World War 1 veteran with a reputation for a fiery temper and a string of murders to his name. This temper gave rise to his 'Wild Bill' nickname.

His mother wanted him to become a priest in the Irish tradition but, having grown up on Catherine Street on the Lower East Side of Manhattan where the Yake Brady Gang taught him how to survive, it was too late for young Bill to turn his morals around.

While a small inconspicuous man to look at, Wild Bill was considered the most vicious killer to head The White Hand Gang. Under his leadership the Mafia was rapidly losing influence to the Irish mob.

His early leadership tenure saw factions still loyal to the deceased Dinny Meehan attempt to exact revenge and kill him. Chaos reigned and lower level White Handers made hits against each other in a tit-for-tat civil war.

His power was consolidated when he joined forces with his future brother-in-law and childhood friend from the Lower East Side, Richard 'Peg Leg' Lonergan. Peace was finally secured for good in 1922 when the Meehan faction's chosen successor, Garry Barry, was found dead, his throat having been slit with a razor. Lovett was finally the undisputed boss of The White Hand Gang.

Although Lovett was on top, he soon wanted out after he married Anna Lonergan, Peg Leg's sister. The Lovetts moved to Ridgefield Park, New Jersey and he ceded day-to-day power to the volatile Peg Leg Lonergan. However, he was still much feared by the Mafia and they wanted him dead.

One night in November 1923, Lovett arranged to meet up with his old buddies from Brooklyn. While he was very drunk at the end of the night, he was shot in the neck and bludgeoned to death. Peg Leg Lonergan was now king of The White Hand Gang but he had not ordered the hit on Wild Bill.

Lovett was assassinated by a Mafioso murder expert nicknamed Dui Cuteddi (Two Knives). He did not use his trademark choice of weapons on this occasion, instead he murdered Lovett with a meat cleaver.

After the hit, Dui Cuteddi was shipped back to Sicily, now a wealthy man with a handsome pension for his services. The murder was ordered by the new, up-and-coming mafia triumvirate of Vince Mangano, Albert Anastasia and Joey Adonis.

The White Hand power passed to 'Peg Leg' Lonergan, a crazed killer who had lost a leg in an accident with a train during a railway looting operation. The full story of Peg Leg Lonergan is explained in more detail in Chapter 10.

By the time the 22-year-old Lonergan took it over in late 1923, The White Hand Gang was a shell of what it was during the Meehan era of the mid-late 19-teens.

Peg Leg viciously began a fightback against Mafia encroachment. He was rabidly anti-Italian and would gleefully maim or kill any Mafia members trying to muscle in on his docklands territory. Woe betide anyone in his territory who would ever pay off the Mafia. He would often beat them up and then demand double tribute from the hapless victims.

However, his two-year leadership would end at the hands of Al Capone when he was murdered in the Adonis Social Club Massacre on Christmas night, 1925.

In December of 1927, a man named Eddie Lynch, a member of the "old Lovett gang" was shot because, as the newspapers at the time reported, he was trying to get the old gang back together again and name himself the leader.

In January of 1928, John 'Non' Connors was shot and killed at a bar on Warren and Bond streets by Helen Finnegan. Connors was said to be the gang's leader, but Ms. Finnegan exerted her own revenge as Connors had killed her brother, James 'The Swede' Finnegan a year earlier.

On November 5, 1928, a man named Eddie McGuire had apparently won leadership of the gang with a roll of the dice and immediately afterwards was shot and killed. Of all The White Hand Gang's leaders, his term was the shortest: five minutes, according to the *Brooklyn Daily Eagle*.

On January 28, 1930 Red Donnelly, a 50-year-old man and veteran of the Meehan era took control and was then killed in a pierhouse on the Columbia Line Pier, shot in the back.

Later in 1930, a man named Jimmy Murray, an old Lovett lieutenant, was shot and left for dead after he named himself leader of the White Handers.

Finally, in 1931, Matty Martin, who had married Anna Lonergan-Lovett a few years after Bill Lovett's murder, was killed after he thought he was owed the leadership of the gang and took control of what was by then nothing more than a collection of drunks and drug addicts.

He was found slumped over a bar stool and was killed, according to reports, due to the declining income of the gang.

By the late 1930s, it was only Anna Lonergan that was still talking about The White Hand Gang's heyday in Brooklyn, though she never spoke nicely of Dinny Meehan since he was an enemy of her first husband, Lovett.

To this day, Bill Lovett is considered the most famous leader of the gang. Richie 'Peg Leg' Lonergan will always be known as having the coolest White Hand Gang moniker and additionally is known for having been killed by Al Capone.

But it was Dinny Meehan who made The White Hand Gang what it was. He was the most organised of the three main leaders and certainly the most consistent. He did what so many other gang leaders failed to do: bring the wild Irish "bhoys" to work as one, and his death in 1920 signalled the beginning of the end of The White Hand Gang.

3

The Westies

WHILE The Gophers cemented the Irish mobsters on the New York criminal landscape, the response to the rise of the Italian mafia and the demise of the Prohibition-era White Hand Gang was the eventual formation of a gang called The Westies.

According to the renowned crime writer TJ Welsh, who wrote the definitive guide to The Westies, *Inside New York's Irish Mob*:

> *"Although never more than twelve to twenty members — depending on who was in or out of jail at any given time — The Westies became synonymous with the last generation of Irish in the birthplace of the Irish Mob."*

The NYPD Organized Crime Squad and the FBI believed The Westies were responsible for 60–100 murders between 1968 and 1986.

At a 1987 press conference announcing the indictment of the gang members, US Attorney Rudolph W. Giuliani noted that The Westies were:

> *"... one of the most savage organizations in the long history of New York gangs."*

So just who were The Westies?

Operating out of New York's Hell's Kitchen, The Westies were an Irish-American organised crime gang. They were involved in racketeering, drug trafficking and very adept at contract killing.

While occasional tensions arose as we will see, The Westies existed alongside the Italian Mafia in Manhattan, working closely with the Gambino crime family and one John Gotti.

Despite its brutal reputation, the populace of Hell's Kitchen lived in relative safety.

The older gangs such as The Gophers and White Handers may have been brutal killers but they believed that their community should not be preyed upon, apart from local businesses who were usually left alone if they paid their requisite protection payment.

However, The Westies had no such qualms, and began to work with the Italian Mafia to wreak havoc on the Hell's Kitchen's population.

The gang has been dubbed The Irish Sopranos and were featured in the 1990 drama *State of Grace*, starring Sean Penn and Gary Oldman, about a man who reunites with a childhood friend who is now a gangster. The gang held court and socialised in the Club 596 and Sunbrite Lounge in Hell's Kitchen.

The Westies have had a turbulent history with many infamous leaders. One was Mickey Spillane and while we look in depth at his life in Chapter 16, it is worth reminding ourselves of the great influence Spillane had over the history of The Westies.

The Spillane leadership, 1962–1977

By the early fifties The Westies gang was in disarray. Most of the senior mobsters had decided to leave the area to escape prosecution. It was into this power vacuum in 1960 that Mickey Spillane established himself as the number 2 and heir apparent to the current Westies leader, Hughie Mulligan.

Spillane was renowned as a gentleman by the people of Hell's Kitchen. He would send flowers to those in hospital and always ensured underprivileged families, of which Hell's Kitchen had a surplus, received turkeys at Thanksgiving.

However, Spillane was no saint and was an accomplished loans shark and adept at the snatch racket, which was kidnapping and holding local business men and members of other criminal gangs for ransom.

Spillane wanted The Westies to move beyond petty crime and establish themselves as rivals to the Italian Mafia. His own family connections would help make this dream a reality.

He married Maureen McManus, daughter of the well-connected McManus family which had controlled the midtown Democratic Party since 1905.

This marriage of political and criminal power allowed The Westies to control access to union jobs and lucrative labour contracts.

The Westies could now move away from the declining Manhattan waterfront and into the more attractive construction rackets, which raked in millions from the New York Coliseum, Madison Square Garden and the Jacob K. Javits Convention Center.

Soon The Westies were earning many millions that made the Mafia envious.

The Genovese crime family resented the fact The Westies had control of the construction sector and decided to act to attempt to wrest control of the Jacob K. Javits Convention Center from The Westies.

War now broke out between the Italian and Irish mobs. Despite the fact that the Italians had more soldiers on the streets, the Irish, using Spillane's guile and creative leadership, came out on top in a brutal conflict. They retained control of the Convention Center and Hell's Kitchen.

The Genovese leadership now decided to turn to an old enemy of Spillane, a man who wanted to become the head of The Westies crime outfit himself, Jimmy Coonan.

Coonan and Spillane had been enemies for many years. Spillane had snatched Coonan's father John, a local accountant, and held him for ransom.

Despite the money being paid, John Coonan was pistol-whipped and severely beaten before returning to his family. An 18-year-old Coonan swore revenge against Spillane and vowed to kill him.

In 1966 he fired a sub machine gun at Spillane and his lieutenants from atop a tenement building in Hell's Kitchen.

It was a comedic attempt at an assassination — despite the high velocity weapon, no one was hit.

Spillane decided Coonan was someone to watch, but being an old fashioned mobster, he did not take action against Coonan, but instead went to his father, beat him up and told him to get his son under control. This enraged Coonan further, but he did not have time to act.

Coonan was imprisoned for a short period of time because of murder and kidnapping charges that were pleaded down to a Class C Manslaughter Felony Charge.

He was released in late 1971 and continued his war with The Westies and his criminal career as part of the Gambino mafia family, who wanted to move in on the Hell's Kitchen area.

In 1977 Spillane was assassinated by Roy DeMeo, a hitman associated with the Gambino crime family. The hit was set up by Jimmy Coonan who was now ready to take over The Westies.

He had informed the Gambino family that he would be more amenable for an alliance than Spillane.

DeMeo was the instrument for his coup and Jimmy Coonan was now the boss of The Westies gang.

The Coonan leadership, 1977–1988

After his release from prison in 1971, Coonan began his war against Spillane. Anyone who stood in his way was subject to a level of intimidation not seen since the days of Prohibition. Coonan noticed a 24-year-old Vietnam vet with a violent temper, Mickey Featherstone, who began to drink in The Westies' Club 596. He decided this was a man who could help him win the war against Spillane.

As in any war, people had to choose sides. Anyone in Hell's Kitchen who took Spillane's side was beaten and even kidnapped. Business owners still paying protection money to Spillane's faction would soon find themselves subject to vandalism and robberies from Coonan's men.

These were a younger generation of Irish mobsters with no regard for people or property, only focused on taking over Hell's Kitchen to fulfil their leader's obsession.

Urban myths have grown around their brutality, that they cut off victims' fingers as trophies and once rolled a rival's severed head down the bar of Club 596. The stories are gruesome but they perhaps have some truth given the enthusiastic vigour the Coonan gang went about their business in the war with Spillane.

Soon most of the population of Hell's Kitchen chose Coonan's side and with the death of Spillane his power was now complete.

The Westies then became closely aligned to the Gambino family under the control of Paul Castellano. This was partly as payback for the Mafia assistance in the assassination of Micky Spillane outside his apartment on May 13, 1977.

Violence and cunning had been Coonan's path to the top of The Westies who, during his tenure, gained a reputation for a level of viciousness that was way above anything previously employed by Irish-American gangsters.

Not only did they dominate the drug, extortion, gambling and loan sharking rackets, they also became the Gambino family's hit squad of choice.

This level of violence was nothing new to Coonan. Mickey Featherstone was now Coonan's bodyguard and favoured enforcer.

In his youth Coonan had worked for a well-known loan shark by the name of Ruby Stein. The Westies, including the older Coonan, now owed a large amount to Stein.

The Westies decided not to pay back their debts but eliminate the loan shark.

Stein was duly murdered, dismembered and his body parts thrown into the Hudson River.

However, the young Westies had not yet mastered the criminal art of making a corpse disappear and had forgotten to pierce the victim's lungs before throwing the torso in to the river.

Stein's torso washed up a few days later and was identified, but no one was ever charged for the murder, however, everyone knew who had been responsible.

The authorities, appalled by the increasing levels of violence, began to crack down on The Westies, but convictions were hard to secure.

In 1979 both Featherstone and Coonan were arrested for the murder of a bartender named Harold Whitehead. The pair were acquitted in December 1979 after one witness mysteriously killed himself and another refused to testify. Jimmy McElroy, another high ranking member of The Westies, was acquitted of the murder of a Teamster in 1980.

However, the authorities would not give up and both Coonan and Featherstone would be imprisoned in 1980.

Coonan was convicted of weapons charges and sentenced to four years in federal prison. Featherstone was incarcerated for counterfeiting. He had been caught after using fake money in a massage parlour. He was convicted on the evidence of a prostitute who remembered seeing his name tattooed on his forearm.

Featherstone, who had been medically discharged from the army after suffering hallucinations, spent his time in prison as a patient on the psychiatric ward of the medical centre for federal prisoners in Springfield, Missouri.

Despite losing their leader and his right-hand man, The Westies continued their catalogue of crime and the gambling, numbers rackets and union racketeering continued, directed by Coonan from behind bars. After his release he resumed full power and his connections with the Gambino crime family grew stronger.

His old friend and associate Roy DeMeo had been murdered and his new Mafia partner was a high ranking Gambino boss, John Gotti, who would go on to head the family after ordering the murder of Gambino Godfather Paul Castellano in December 1985.

The Westies were now being used as the muscle of the Gambino family and while the money flowed in, one man was not happy.

Coonan's bodyguard Michael Featherstone was a proud Irishman and Westie. He resented the authority the Gambinos and the control John Gotti held over Coonan and The Westies.

Featherstone saw this emasculation of The Westies as a betrayal of all the Irish-Americans in Hell's Kitchen.

This led to a major falling out with Coonan who decided that Featherstone was too volatile an enemy to have around. In a strange show of mercy he decided not to have him murdered, but instead framed for murder.

Coonan authorised the hit of mobster Michael Holly. A Westie we shall hear more of by the name of Billy Bokun disguised himself as Mickey Featherstone. This led to the arrest of Featherstone on a murder charge.

Featherstone was convicted in March 1986 and sentenced to 25 years in prison. He knew he had been set up and he knew it was Coonan who had set him up. He approached his prosecutors and gave them a proposal. He offered to turn informant in return for quashing his conviction and his freedom.

He arranged for his wife Sissy to record conversations that would incriminate Coonan and other members of The Westies.

In September 1986, the prosecutor who oversaw

Featherstone's initial murder conviction informed Judge Alvin Schlesinger that post-conviction investigations had revealed Featherstone was in fact innocent. The judge immediately overturned the verdict.

Featherstone's information and the recordings provided by his wife ensured the arrest of Coonan and a whole slate of Westie gang members on charges ranging from murder to other serious crimes.

Federal prosecutor Rudolph Giuliani then invoked the Racketeer Influenced and Corrupt Organizations Indictment, commonly referred to as the RICO Act or simply RICO. This was a United States federal law, that provides for extended criminal penalties and a civil cause of action for acts performed as part of an ongoing criminal organisation.

Coonan was now in deep trouble. Not only did Giuliani have the recordings, he now had a special witness as Featherstone turned informant against his old friend and fellow Westie.

Featherstone testified in open court for four weeks in the trial that began in September 1987 and concluded with major convictions in 1988.

Coonan was sentenced to 75 years in prison with no possibility for parole.

Other leading Westie members were also sentenced to long prison terms, including James McElroy, a top enforcer who was sentenced to 60 years, and Richard 'Mugsy' Ritter, a career criminal sentenced to 40 years on loan-sharking and drug-related charges.

As for Featherstone, he pleaded guilty to a charge of Racketeering and was sentenced to five years. Due to his co-operation this was suspended and he walked out of court and straight into a witness protection programme.

The incarceration of Coonan and other gang members dealt a bitter blow to The Westies but this was not yet fatal and others now stepped forward to lead the gang. One such man was Bosko Radonjich.

The Bosko Radonjich leadership, 1988–1992

Bosko Radonjich was born in 1943 in Užice in what is now modern Serbia but which at the time of his birth was in Yugoslavia.

Bosko's father was executed by Tito's communist forces, this was because he belonged to the Chetnik forces of Draža Mihailović. The Chetniks were a Serbian nationalist guerrilla force that formed during World War II to resist the Axis invaders and Croatian collaborators but that primarily fought a civil war against the Yugoslav communist guerrillas.

As a Serbian nationalist in Communist Yugoslavia, life was not easy. Bosko resolved to move to the US and in 1970 he was smuggled across the border into Austria with the help of his friend and Red Star Belgrade footballer, Milovan Đorić.

Bosko was smuggled to freedom on the team bus heading for Graz and he finally reached the US via a short stay in Austria and Italy.

Radonjich settled in the Hell's Kitchen area of Manhattan. Not yet a Westie, he joined the Serbian Homeland Liberation Movement (SOPO). This was a fervently anti-communist terrorist group headed by his close friend the anti-communist and Serbian royalist, Nikola Kavaja.

Bosko was now on the radar of the UDBA, the Yugoslav state security services — and for good reason.

In 1975, Radonjich took part in a bombing at the Yugoslav mission to the United Nations in which no one was hurt. In 1978, he plead guilty to conspiracy charges in the 1975 Chicago bombing of a Yugoslavian consul's home and for plotting to bomb a Yugoslav social club in the city.

Radonjich was released in 1982 and back in Hell's Kitchen now joined The Westies as a close associate of gang leader, Jimmy Coonan.

When The Westies leadership was decimated as part of the Featherstone revelations in 1988, Bosko seized control.

He received the blessing and support of John Gotti, now the boss of the Gambino crime family. This was because Gotti owed Radonjich who was instrumental in helping Gotti tamper with the jury in his initial racketeering trial in 1986.

Under Bosko, The Westies operated a lucrative burglary ring. This was led by Brian Bentley and was very successful until it was broken up in 1992.

The heat was now on The Westies and highly publicised investigations by the District Attorney's Office made Radonjich very nervous. With Gotti now in jail for life, the district attorney's chief investigator, Michael G Cherkasky, now had enough ammunition to indict him on jury-tampering charges as the first step to a more aggressive plethora of charges.

Rather than face prosecution, Radonjich fled the US in 1992 and returned to Serbia where he opened a nightclub.

During the Bosnian war he became a close adviser to Radovan Karadžić, the Bosnian Serb leader who would later be charged with war crimes.

He would not return to the US until 1999, when he was soon arrested in Miami Florida on charges of jury tampering for John Gotti.

This related to the Gotti trial in the late eighties. Radonjich had a friend on the jury, a certain George Pape. He let it be known that he was willing to sell his vote to help acquit Gotti.

Sammy the Bull Gravano, a Gambino capo and close friend of Gotti, arranged for Radonjich to pay Pape $60k to guarantee at least a hung jury. The trial collapsed.

Pape was later convicted for this in 1992 and sentenced to three years in prison.

Ironically, the main witness in the case against Radonjich was Gotti's long-time associate and the man whose evidence had helped put him behind bars, Sammy the Bull Gravano.

However, Gravano had just been arrested for drug-related offences and Radonjich's attorney attested that his testimony was now suspect and he was an unreliable witness. The judge agreed.

As the entire case against him was his word against Gravano, the charges were dropped. He was released from custody in March 2001 and left for Serbia and again opened a nightclub.

In 2003 the Serbian Prime Minister Zoran Đinđić was assassinated and as part of the investigation Radonjich again found himself arrested but was released after three days.

Radonjich spent the rest of his life running various bars and clubs and died following a brief illness on March 31, 2011.

So, what of The Westies? Well, eventually gentrification caused many of the working class to move out of Hell's Kitchen, and the city government, in its efforts to clean New York up, even tried to rename Hell's Kitchen, although their efforts have not quite succeeded.

While official signs and transportation maps point to Clinton Hill, residents and the public still refer to the area by its old name.

When Michael G. Cherkasky, chief of the Investigations Division of the District Attorney's Office, was asked how much still remained of The Westies, he said: "Too much," and that perhaps "it's not the end" of the gang.

While Capone and his bodyguard were drinking downstairs, the North Siders drove their cars by the lobby and opened fire with their Thompson submachine guns

4

The Chicago
North Side Gang

BY 1860 Chicago was the fourth largest city in America, after New York, Boston and Philadelphia.

The Irish had been in Chicago in large numbers from 1830 onwards but the population rapidly grew for two distinctly different factors.

The first was the influx of Irish navvies and their families to help build the Illinois and Michigan canal, which started in 1836. On its completion, the workers moved to the lumber wharves, rail roads and steel mills which were powering the phenomenal growth of Chicago from a frontier town to an economic powerhouse and urban metropolis.

The second was that this economic prosperity coincided with the tragedy of 'An Gorta Mór', the great Irish famine, which drove millions to their death or emigration. Chicago proved to be a beacon for many who fled the hungry glens and hills of Ireland.

Not settled until the 1800s Chicago was a new city in comparison to the other Irish refuges of Boston, New York and Philadelphia. This meant that while the Chicago Irish did suffer a level of discrimination and prejudice, this was nothing like the Anti Catholic and Anti Irish campaigns from native born Non Catholic Americans that raged throughout the eastern seaboard.

The newness of Chicago and the fact it did not have the ingrained institutions and structures of other cities, meant it was indeed a land of opportunity for emigrants and many Irish quickly established themselves successfully in a myriad of areas, such as commerce, politics and eventually crime.

The most successful Irish crime syndicate was The North Side Gang, which evolved as the Irish response to the growing power of the Italian mafia in Chicago led by Johnny Torrio and Al Capone. The Italian mafia became known as the Chicago Outfit and controlled most of the criminal activities in the city, with a vice-like grip and a high level of brutality.

Johnny Torrio was the figurehead and Al Capone was the blunt weapon. Capone had ironically been moved from New York for his own safety, as he was a target for the Irish American Hell's Kitchen-based White Hand Gang. For this reason alone, it is safe to say he had little time for Irish crime gangs, especially the growing North Side Gang.

The North Side Gang was the brainchild of three men — George 'Deanie' O'Banion and his childhood friends Earl 'Hymie' Weiss and George 'Bugs' Moran. O'Banion would be the North Side Gang's first leader. A more in-depth analysis of O'Banion's life is covered in Chapter 14.

Known as Deanie, O'Banion was Chicago's most well-known Irish gangster. He grew up in poverty and had a tragic childhood, eventually becoming a feared murderer. He was a man with a complex character; in one pocket could be found a revolver and in the other a set of Rosary beads.

While a violent and ruthless killer, he had a bizarre hobby flower arranging.

He loved flowers so much, a throwback to his childhood, that he established a flower shop on North State Street. This was not only the headquarters of The North Side Gang but a thriving business, where O'Banion would soon become known as the florist to the mob.

It was also the place where O'Banion met his maker when he was murdered by Chicago outfit hoods in 1924 in revenge for a business deal gone sour.

The North Side Gang evolved from the Market Street gang, one of the many small-time street gangs that plagued the Irish-American suburbs of Chicago.

Operating out of Chicago's 42nd and 43rd wards, the Market Street boys were renowned in the craft of street crime — pick-pocketing, petty crime and extortion.

They were soon employed by unscrupulous employers as Strike breakers and to discourage union activity. This was known as 'labour slugging'. They soon joined the Chicago newspaper circulation wars of the early 1910s between the *Chicago Examiner* and the *Chicago Tribune*.

Each publication would hire street gangs to beat up newsstand owners who did not carry their publication or wreck the stands of rival papers. It was not unknown for gangs to work for both publications, sometimes at the same time.

When Prohibition began, O'Banion, 'Hymie' Weiss and 'Bugs' Moran quickly took control of the existing breweries and whiskey distilleries in the north side of Chicago. They also made alliances with brewers in Canada. This allowed them to establish a virtual monopoly on safe illegal alcohol. They were able to supply and sell real beer and high quality whiskey.

Their initial rivals soon fell by the wayside as they could only produce what became known as rotgut liquor, which could not only cause illness but often blind a drinker.

Working out of McGovern's Saloon and Café, The North Side Gang totally controlled the working class 42nd and 43rd wards. Boot-legging was not the only activity undertaken, local businesses had to pay tribute and gambling was a massive part of the gang's income. One thing they would not do was prostitution. This was down to O'Banion's devout Roman Catholic faith, which did not preclude brutal murders, but ensured he would not allow prostitution in his territory.

O'Banion strengthened his political protection by helping his politician friends commit election fraud. The North Side Gang also enjoyed considerable protection from the Chicago police department. In 1924, Chicago police assisted The North Side Gang in robbing the Sibly Distillery, which had been under federal guard since the beginning of Prohibition.

In early 1924, O'Banion agreed to an alliance with Torrio and Capone, however, this began to deteriorate when O'Banion offered to sell Torrio the valuable Sieben Brewery.

On May 19, 1924, while Torrio was inspecting the property, O'Banion arranged for the police to raid the place and arrest Torrio. After his release from custody,

Torrio acceded to demands from the Italian mobsters for O'Banion to die.

On November 10, three unidentified men entered the Schofield Flower Shop owned by O'Banion and shot him dead. This was to be the beginning of a five-year gang war between The North Side Gang against the Chicago outfit.

The Chicago gang war

While the death of O'Banion rocked The North Side Gang, they were still in a very strong position and they decided to form a governing council with Hymie Weiss as their leader.

Hymie Weiss was born Henry Earl J Wojciechowski in present day Poland and grew up a childhood friend of O'Banion in Chicago's north side. Though not Irish and despite his Jewish sounding name, he was a Roman Catholic and thus acceptable to the members of The North Side Gang.

Weiss had been a lifelong friend of O'Banion and was devastated at his death and wanted revenge.

The North Side Gang immediately struck back at the man they knew had ordered the killing of O'Banion, Al Capone. On January 12, 1925 Weiss, Bugs Moran and Vincent Drucci attempted to murder Capone while he was eating in a Chicago restaurant.

As Capone left, The North Side Gang fired at Capone's car. While they wounded his chauffeur, Sylvester Barton, Capone survived unharmed but deeply shaken.

It was after this attempted hit that Capone arranged for his famous armoured car to be created.

On January 24, shortly after the assassination attempt on Capone had taken place, Weiss, Moran, and Drucci ambushed the nominal head of the Chicago outfit Johnny Torrio as he returned from shopping with his wife.

Both Torrio and his chauffeur Robert Barton were wounded several times. As Moran was about to kill Torrio, the gun misfired; the gang members were forced to flee the scene as the police arrived.

A shocked Torrio already in semi-retirement decided he wanted out all together and passed official leadership of the Chicago Outfit to Al Capone.

Weiss and the North Siders then went after the Genna Family, allies of the Chicago Outfit.

After their leadership was decimated the remaining members of the Genna family fled Chicago and The North Side Gang took over their bootlegging operation.

Emboldened, Weiss and Moran decided to go after Capone again. In the second attack on Capone, a fleet of North Side cars, with Moran in the lead car, drove to Capone's hotel in the Mafia-controlled area of Cicero, a town outside Chicago.

While Capone and his bodyguard were drinking downstairs, the North Siders drove their cars by the lobby and opened fire with their Thompson submachine guns.

As the bullets flew all around, Capone and his bodyguard dived to the floor. Once again he survived the hit but was now clearly rattled and wanted a truce.

He sent word to Weiss and Moran that he wanted a ceasefire. A truce was made but this was just a cover for Capone whose pride was hurt. He wanted revenge.

The truce ended in a matter of weeks when Capone arranged for his men to brutally gun down Hymie Weiss and several associates.

With Weiss dead, Vincent Drucci and Moran now assumed joint leadership of The North Side Gang. The two sides traded killings and bombings for several more months until a peace conference was held.

Moran and Capone both appeared at the meeting, along with many other mob bosses.

During the conference, Capone complained that "they were making a shooting gallery of a great business". He also stated that:

"Chicago should be seen as a pie and each gang gets a slice of the pie."

The two gangs agreed to make peace. This peace would last for a while. No killings occurred that were a result of gang war. Vincent Drucci was killed during this time, but it resulted from a brawl with police. Moran now became the sole boss of The North Side Gang.

However, conflict eventually started again. Moran would regularly hijack Capone's beer shipments, naturally aggravating Capone.

Capone retaliated by burning down Moran's dog track. A few days later, Capone's own dog track went up in smoke. Moran was the prime suspect.

Open warfare started again between the two gangs. Moran ordered the execution of two union leaders who were powerful allies and personal friends of Capone. This act prompted Capone to order what would now become known as the St Valentine's Day Massacre.

On February 14, 1929, four men — two dressed as police officers — entered a garage at 2122 North Clark Street, in the Lincoln Park neighbourhood of Chicago's north side. This was a known hangout for The North Side Gang.

They proceeded to order the six gang members and one of their friends to stand against the wall. Thinking this was a police raid, they obliged. The intruders then proceeded to fire around 70 bullets into them from hand guns and a submachine gun.

Six of the men died instantly, and when genuine police officers from Chicago's 36th district turned up they found only one survivor amongst the carnage.

Frank 'Tight Lips' Gusenberg was barely alive. In the few minutes that he lived, the police tried to get him to reveal what had happened, but Frank — true to his nickname — said nothing.

However, the primary target of the gunmen, Bugs Moran, was not at the garage and escaped harm.

Police could find only a few eyewitnesses, but eventually concluded that gunmen dressed as police officers had entered the garage and pretended to be arresting the men. Though Moran and others immediately blamed the massacre on Capone's gang, the famous gangster himself claimed to have been at his home in Florida at the time. No one was ever brought to trial for the murders.

The St Valentine's Day Massacre now left the war in a stalemate.

The publicity surrounding the brutality of the crime resulted in a Federal crackdown on all gang activity in Chicago that would eventually lead to the downfall of both Moran and Al Capone.

Although Bugs Moran survived the St. Valentine's Day Massacre, several experienced North Side gunmen had been lost.

The North Side Gang continued to control the 42nd and 43rd Wards and managed to thwart a takeover attempt by Frank McErlane, an associate of Al Capone in 1930.

As the decade progressed, the power of The North Side Gang slowly declined. Moran and The North Side Gang eventually lost control of their gambling operations to the new Mafia-controlled National Crime Syndicate.

In a bid to make money, Moran reverted to his earlier Market Street days and returned to petty crime. On April 30, 1939, Moran was convicted of conspiracy to make and cash $62,000 worth of American Express checks. He was not released until December 21, 1943. Seventeen years after being one of the richest gangsters in Chicago, Moran was now almost penniless.

On July 6, 1946, Moran was arrested for his involvement in a June 28, 1945, robbery of a tavern in Dayton, Ohio. He was found guilty and sentenced to 20 years in Ohio State prison. On his release and desperate for money, he again resorted to robbery and was sentenced to a 10-year stretch in Leavenworth prison in Kansas.

George Bugs Moran died only a few months later of lung cancer on February 25, 1957 at the age of 63.

The last of the great leaders of The North Side Gang was dead.

The Winter Hill Gang were an Irish-American federation of street gangs that grew into a sophisticated money-making machine that took on the might of the Italian Mafia

5

The Boston Winter Hill Gang

THE Irish have been in Boston since colonial times, when they arrived as indentured servants, merchants, sailors, or tradesmen.

According to the well-known historian James Cullen, a large number of Irish immigrants arrived as early as 1654, on the ship Goodfellow, and were "sold" into indentured servitude "to such of the inhabitants as needed them."

A fresh wave of Irish immigration to Boston started in the 1820s. Initially most of the newcomers were Protestants, but increasingly they were joined by Roman Catholics.

During the Famine, the port of Boston was a major centre of immigration and by 1850, the Irish were the largest ethnic group in Boston.

Most of the immigrants during this period were poor, unskilled labourers from rural backgrounds who settled in the slums of the North End, the South Cove, and Fort Hill. Many were not only destitute but weakened by typhus contracted on the coffin ships that had brought them across the Atlantic.

Today, with some 23 percent of Boston's population claiming Irish ancestry and many holding positions of power and influence in politics, society and industry, the city retains its place as a centre of Irish-American culture and history.

Boston has a well-chronicled history of Irish mob activity, particularly in the heavily Irish-American neighbourhoods like Somerville, Charlestown, South Boston ("Southie"), Dorchester and Roxbury where the earliest Irish gangs arose during Prohibition.

Frank Wallace of the Gustin gang dominated Boston's underworld until his death in 1931, when he was ambushed by Italian gangsters in the North End. Numerous gang wars between rival Irish gangs during the early and mid-20th century would contribute to their decline.

The most famous of these gangs and arguably the most effective was The Winter Hill Gang.

They were an Irish-American federation of street gangs that grew into a sophisticated money-making machine that took on the might of the Italian Mafia. They took their name from the Winter Hill area of Somerville Massachusetts north of Boston.

The name was first used by journalists from the *Boston Herald* in the early 1970s.

Its members included a who's who of notorious Boston gangsters such as Howie Winter, James 'Buddy' McLean, James J. 'Whitey' Bulger, and hitmen John Martorano and Stephen 'The Rifleman' Flemmi. They were most influential from 1965 under the rule of McLean and Winter until the takeover led by Whitey Bulger in 1979, who is covered in more depth in Chapter 22.

The Winter Hill Gang carried out a whole range of

criminal activities but are best known for fixing horse races in the north-eastern United States and shipping weapons to the Irish Republican Army.

Their brutal rise to the top in Boston was a result of a vicious war fought against the McLaughlin Gang of Charlestown, led by Bernie McLaughlin from 1961 until 1967.

James 'Buddy' McLean was the leader of The Winter Hill Gang during this conflict.

The two gangs had enjoyed success without coming into conflict for a number of years until a minor altercation suddenly got out of hand.

Both gangs had members at a party in Salisbury Beach on Labour Day 1961. Georgie McLaughlin, brother of Bernie, took a shine to the girlfriend of a Winter Hill Gang member, Alex 'Bobo' Petricone JR.

This was an unwanted advance and McLaughlin was taken outside, badly beaten by Winter Hill gang members and dumped outside the local hospital.

Bernie McLaughlin wanted revenge and went to see 'Buddy' McLean and demanded that he hand over the members of the gang who had beaten his brother.

McLean, whilst not wishing a war, steadfastly refused.

The McLaughlins took this refusal as an insult and attempted to wire a bomb to McLean's wife's car.

Enraged, McLean shot and killed McLaughlin coming out of the Morning Glory bar in Charlestown, Massachusetts in October 1961. This was the start of the infamous Boston Irish gang war.

An interesting side note to the incident is that during the war Alex 'Bobo' Petricone JR. fled the Boston area to move to Los Angeles to be an actor. He changed his name to Alex Rocco and is best known for playing the character of gangster Moe Green in the *Godfather* movies.

Over the next few years The Winter Hill Gang would go on to kill and maim virtually all of the McLaughlin gang members. In 1965 one of the few remaining McLaughlin foot soldiers, Steve Hughes, shot and killed Buddy McLean.

Howie Winters assumed control of the gang and set out to avenge his friend. Shortly after the last remaining McLaughlin brother nicknamed Punchy was shot while waiting for a bus in the West Roxbury section of Boston.

Buddy McLean's killer, Steve Hughes along with his brother Connie, were shot and killed in 1966 by hitman Frank Salemne.

The Winter Hill Gang had won the Boston gang wars and were now the preeminent Irish crime syndicate, not only in Boston but in the entire New England area.

In the book *Black Mass* by Dick Lehr and Gerard O'Neill, the authors claimed that The Winter Hill Gang were far more feared and powerful than their rivals, the Boston branch of the Patriarca crime family run by the Angiulo brothers.

While brutal killers, The Winter Hill Gang did not have the expertise to profit in the long term. Yes, they could easily kill rivals to take over their rackets, but they showed over time that they had no idea how to run them.

By 1977 Howie Winters and his associate John Martorano were going broke. Eventually they had to go to Patriarca family underboss Gennaro Anguilo to borrow money.

To make the weekly payments, they began going into businesses with people they didn't know and couldn't trust. These activities included rigging horse races and drug-trafficking. It was the decision to involve outsiders with their business that led to their downfall.

By 1979, Howie Winter and the rest of the Somerville crew were all sent to prison for fixing horse races, leaving Whitey Bulger and Stephen Flemmi as the new leaders of The Winter Hill Gang.

As the years went by, James Bulger and Steven Flemmi lost interest in running any kind of gambling operation. They would eventually only provide protection for bookmakers, drug dealers and truck hijackers.

By 1991, even as Bulger's criminal career was winding down, he remained the undisputed mob boss. His criminal associate Kevin Weeks was not considered a threat, and neither were John Shea, Eddie Mac, 'Polecat' Moore or John Cherry.

Boston journalist Howie Carr commented:

"They hadn't really been gangsters so much as they'd been ex-boxers and bar-room brawlers who had become cocaine dealers."

One problem that arose with the gang was that they enjoyed partaking in their own vices.

Like their customers, they spent afternoons in the bars drinking beer and watching professional football on television, often doubling up wagers on late West Coast games as they desperately tried to break even and chased their losses.

In 1998, during a trial for racketeering and fixing horse races, Steve Flemmi and Whitey Bulger were revealed under disclosure, to be FBI informants. Both men were implicated in many unlawful activities, including murder, but were never brought to justice due to their FBI handlers diverting their guilt onto others in the gang or various other gangs of the time.

They not only ratted out other gangs, but they did so to their own brothers in The Winter Hill Gang. When they had nothing to report to the FBI, they would make up information to ensure that they were still seen to be high value informers. This false information would often result in the arrest of Winter Hill members, set up by their own leaders.

However the good times were soon over. In 1995, Bulger and Stephen Flemmi were indicted. Bulger, however, managed to evade capture. According to the authorities, Bulger's FBI handler and longtime friend, Special Agent John Connelly, tipped Bulger off to the 1995 indictment, allowing Whitey to escape with his then girlfriend, Theresa Stanley. This was not the end of Whitey Bulger but it was the end of The Winter Hill Gang.

6

John Morrissey
Boxer, Gang Boss
and US Congressman

IRISH-American Congressman John Morrissey, once told the US House of Representatives during a heated debate:

> "I have been a wharf rat, chicken thief, prize fighter, gambler, and member of Congress and if any gentleman on the other side wants his constitution amended, just let him step into the Rotunda with me."

This was no ideal threat, because as we shall see, John Morrissey was a man who rose from humble beginnings to the top of New York society and American politics using his fists and intellect in equal measure.

Born in Temple, Co Tipperary on February 12, 1831, John Morrissey would soon leave his native Ireland with his parents bound for the United States. In early 1831, his family settled in the town of Troy in New York State.

The young Morrissey didn't spend much time in any formal schooling. In his early teens, due to his massive physique, which made him look much older than he was, he found himself working as a bouncer in a Troy brothel.

It was here that, in between sorting out wayward clients, Morrissey taught himself how to read and write.

Realising his future was limited in Troy, it was not long before a young John Morrissey was drawn to the Irish-American enclaves of New York City itself.

Not much is known of Morrissey's early life, but he later recounted that he spent his teens learning to fight in bar rooms and on the gambling riverboats, that frequented the New York wharfs.

Later in life his political enemies would claim that as a youth he had been indicted twice for burglary, once for assault and battery, and once for assault with intent to kill.

Along with many other young men of Irish descent, Morrissey joined the Irish street gang, the Dead Rabbits. Their emblem, a rabbit impaled upon a staff, was carried into their wild street fights, hoisted proudly as a flag of war. Morrissey's physique and prowess in brutal street fights as part of the gang, convinced him to pursue a career as a professional prize-fighter as well as a criminal enforcer.

Friends would later recount that he had his first fight in Captain Isaiah Rynders saloon, at 28 Park Row.

Captain Rynder worked for the Tammany Hall Democratic party faction. His job was to arrange general mayhem and ballot-box stuffing to ensure victory for the right candidate. He was always on the lookout for young men with fighting skills and he found one in John Morrissey.

Tammany Hall, or simply Tammany, was the name given to a powerful political machine that essentially ran New York City throughout much of the 19th century.

The organisation reached a peak of notoriety in the decade following the Civil War, when it harboured 'The Ring', the corrupted political organisation of William Magear Tweed, known as 'Boss Tweed'.

Tammany Hall was the archetype of the political machines that flourished in many American cities in the late 1800s and early 1900s.

The influence of Tammany did not wane until the 1930s, and the organisation itself did not cease to exist until the 1960s.

Morrissey would soon be part of this Tammany machine. When organising a local illegal bare-knuckle fight, Captain Rynder asked if any prize fighters were present in his bar.

A young John Morrissey took off his cap, and said:

"I can lick any man in the place."

This was soon put to the test, as eight men turned from the bar, grabbed chairs, bottles, and other handy makeshift weapons, and came at Morrissey determined to test this confident boast.

Nonetheless, Morrissey held his own, until Rynder hit him under the ear with a spittoon he found close by, to rescue him from the ensuing mayhem.

The Captain paid Morrissey's medical bills and then employed him in the Tammany political operation as a "shoulder-hitter" (a fighter who enforced the will of a political boss by intimidation or violence).

Morrissey met Irish immigrants at the dock, found them work and shelter, and after obtaining their pledges to vote for the Democratic Tammany ticket, helped them get American citizenship. He did this by arranging their appearances before sympathetic and well bribed judges.

Morrissey continued his bare knuckle fighting and it was at one such bout that he would earn his lifelong nickname of 'Old Smoke'.

During a fight in the basement of a New York hotel, a stove was overturned spilling hot coals over the floor. The fight continued until Morrissey's opponent, violent street fighter Tom McCann, knocked John to the floor and held him down with his back upon the burning coals.

In agony, John's flesh began to simmer and smoke. His friends came to his assistance, pouring cold water on the embers. Enduring the pain, Morrissey got back up to his feet, and in a blind rage, with his back still smoking, he battered McCann senseless. The watching enthralled bystanders gave him the nickname 'Old Smoke', a name he was to be known by for the rest of his life.

Not yet 20, John Morrissey decided to leave New York and seek his fortune in the Californian gold rush.

Despite finding no luck as a gold prospector, he turned his hand to gambling and was a great success making a fortune winning gold from newly rich and usually drunk prospectors.

However, Morrissey could not escape the lure of the ring and he soon had his first professional fight, knocking out a well-known pugilist, George Thompson, in the 11th round and winning the then princely sum of $5,000.

His pockets now full, Morrissey decided he would return to New York and challenge the current American boxing champion 'Yankee Sullivan' (a native of Bandon, Co Cork whose real name was James Ambrose).

While waiting for Sullivan to agree to fight him, Morrissey continued his involvement in New York politics as an enforcer using his associates in the Dead Rabbits gang as additional muscle.

The fight with 'Yankee Sullivan' was finally arranged for October 12, 1853. Three thousand people gathered in a field in Boston Corner to witness a gruelling but engrossing and illegal bare-knuckle boxing match, with both Irish men fighting for the right to call themselves the undisputed champion of America.

Sullivan was the more technically gifted boxer and for 37 rounds he pummelled and battered Morrissey. He landed so many punches to his face that Old Smokes nose would never regain its original shape.

The bout soon began to take its toll and Morrissey was out on his feet and heading for defeat, but as had happened so many times in his short life, fate would turn in his favour.

As with many bare-knuckle bouts, the fighting was not just contained to the ring as a brawl broke out between the rival supporters and this began to spill into the ring. In the confusion Sullivan didn't hear the bell for the start of round 38 and he failed to leave his corner by the required time. The referee intervened, stopped the fight and awarded the bout to Morrissey.

Battered, bruised and almost unconscious the confused Old Smoke was now the bare-knuckle champion of America. Morrissey proceeded to use his newfound fame and wealth to open a bar and gambling den, which would become famous for cock fights.

He also gained control of the Dead Rabbits and it was now that his infamous rivalry intensified with William Poole, who had the well-earned nickname 'Bill the Butcher', who was famously portrayed by Daniel Day-Lewis in the film *Gangs of New York*.

Working again for Tammany Hall, Morrissey organized the Dead Rabbits to battle Bill the Butchers anti-immigrant American Party, otherwise known as the 'Know Nothing' gang.

The two gangs became enforcers for battling political parties. The Know Nothing anti-immigration party employed William Poole and the Bowery Boys to ensure the ballot boxes gave the right results.

Old Smoke and the Dead Rabbits were hired by the pro-Irish group, Democratic Tammany Hall faction, to ensure Poole and his thugs would not be successful and that Irish immigrants knew which party was looking after their interests.

However, politics alone did not explain the intense rivalry between Morrissey and Bill the Butcher. The violence between the rival gangs intensified and both leaders chose to stage a boxing match. In July 1854, Bill the Butcher defeated Morrissey in the ring.

There was a deep hatred between the men, while Poole had defeated Morrissey in the ring, he would lose a fight to a bullet several months later.

Street fights between the two gangs continued, resulting in the deaths of several members, including the Butcher in March 1855, when two of Morrissey's friends, Lew Baker and Jim Turner, shot and fatally wounded Bill the Butcher at a saloon on Broadway.

Morrissey and Baker were charged with his murder, but they were released as the jury could not reach a verdict. This was hardly surprising as a sizeable proportion of them had been bribed not to.

It is no doubt Morrissey masterminded the death of Bill the Butcher and for his part in facing down Poole's anti-Catholic and anti-immigrant party, the Know-Nothings, he achieved an almost mythical hero status within the local Irish community.

As a reward, the Democratic Tammany Hall faction gave Morrissey the go-ahead to open another gambling house, and also promised that there would be no police interference in the running operations.

With this blank cheque, Old Smoke retired from boxing to concentrate on his growing gambling and brothel empire.

Five years after his 'defeat' of Sullivan, Morrissey emerged from self-imposed retirement to fight John C. Heenan, the son of another Irish family in Troy.

Again, Morrissey's ability to absorb punches allowed him to stay in the ring with a more skilled opponent and when Heenan lost the use of his right hand after hitting it off a corner stake, Old Smoke's endurance paid off and he emerged victorious once more.

Morrissey knew that despite his courage, he had been lucky in the ring and decided to retire and concentrate on his other skills, that of organised crime and gambling.

He eventually owned 16 gambling dens and numerous brothels. Heenan claimed the title on Morrissey's retirement from boxing in 1859.

In 1861, he decided to reinvent himself once again and left New York behind to move to the then small but growing town of Saratoga.

With $700,000 in cash, he underwent an image makeover, changing his ways to suit his new improved status and in the process, becoming a serious political force.

He built a new state-of-the-art and plush casino called the Club House, which counted Civil War generals like Sherman and Grant among its regular clients.

He invested his money wisely and profitably in real estate and in 1863 opened the Saratoga Springs racing track which is still in use to this day.

Always conscious of his past though, Morrissey kept his own name off all official documents when opening Saratoga Racecourse in 1864. He knew that his past would come back to haunt him and impact on the success of his new venture. He wisely appointed William Travers, a respected figure in the horse-breeding world, as the venue's first president.

Saratoga racecourse is still thriving to this day and it is Travers, not Morrissey, who is commemorated in its flagship race every August.

Now a wealthy man and reinventing his life story, airbrushing his Dead Rabbit and brothel-owning past, Morrissey turned his eye towards politics. However, this time he would not be an enforcer but the candidate. His wealth and party machine would ensure he would be elected twice to the US congress as a Democratic member.

His transformation became so complete that the writer Elliot J Gorn in his book, *The Manly Art; Bare-knuckle Prize Fighting in America*', said of him:

> "As a politician, Morrissey maintained arms-length contact with the gangs, brothels, and saloons of his youth, and his rough personal manner had become quiet, even genteel."

In early 1870, before revelations of Tammany Hall corruption became public, Morrissey joined a faction called the Young Democracy that revolted against Tammany Hall's leader Boss Tweed's authoritarian rule.

Tweed, however, learned of their plot to unseat him as head of Tammany Hall, and used policemen to prevent the Young Democracy members from entering the building on the night of their planned coup.

The rebel organisation quickly folded, and Morrissey grew tired of the rampant corruption in Tammany Hall and left Congress after his second term.

Morrissey eventually testified against Boss Tweed and helped put him in prison. In 1875, now reinvigorated politically, Morrissey stood for a seat in the New York State legislature, beating his Tammany Hall opponent to win the right to represent Boss Tweed's old district. Old Smoke had taken full revenge.

His critics taunted him that he could only have been elected in such a safe precinct. A proud man, he then ran in 1877 and won in a new district, defeating another Tammany politician, August Schell.

In May 1878, only a few months into his second legislative term, Morrissey contracted pneumonia and died on May 1, 1878 at the age of 47.

Old Smoke was held in such high esteem that on the day of his funeral, the New York State closed all its public offices and the flags were flown at half-mast.

Twenty thousand mourners lined the streets to pay their last respects and the entire New York State Senate attended his funeral. He was buried in St. Peter's Cemetery, just outside Troy.

Not bad for a boy from Templemore, who used his wits and fists to rise from poverty to become a US Congressman.

Most newspapers praised the former pugilist, gambler, gang leader, brothel owner and politician on his death, with one report observing:

"That he had transcended his rowdy youth to become a useful citizen, a man of shrewdness, rectitude, and generosity."

In 1996 he was elected in to the International Boxing Hall of Fame, so the legend of 'Old Smoke' — boxer, gang boss and US Congressman — lives on to this day.

7

Emmet Dalton
The Hollywood Outlaw

EMMET DALTON was a cowboy, a lawman, bank robber, author and eventually a minor Hollywood celebrity. Not many Irish immigrants in America could make those claims.

Emmet Dalton was born on May 3, 1871, just outside Belton Missouri, the eleventh child of Irish immigrants Lewis and Adeline Dalton. The Emmet family would produce farmers, lawmen and bank robbers.

In 1883, the family moved to Vinita in the Indian Territory. Four years later Emmet began working as a cowboy at the Bar X ranch in Triangle country. It was there that he first encountered Bill Power and Dick Broadwell who would later become members of the infamous Dalton gang.

The Dalton family were not yet involved in criminal activity. In fact, the opposite was true, as Emmet's brother Frank was working as a US Marshall and his other brother and close friend Bob Dalton was his deputy. Sadly Frank would die a hero's death at the hands of whiskey runners in November 1887.

Frank was buried in Coffeyville, Kansas. The Dalton

family moved to just outside town to be close to the grave. Coffeyville would have a dramatic impact on Emmet, but that's for later in the story.

Emmett's older brother Gratton, known as Grat, returned from living with his eldest living brother Bill in California and became a US Deputy alongside his other brother Bob. It was not long before Emmet joined his brothers as their posseman.

Given their subsequent life of crime, it's ironic that the historical records state that the Daltons were considered good law officers. They are described in numerous sources as 'brave, friendly and polite'. However, this would soon change.

Emmett had always looked up to his older brother Bob who many described as having a wild and reckless streak.

The Dalton boys' career in law enforcement came to an end in March 1890 when Bob and Emmett were arrested on a charge of introducing intoxicating liquor into the Indian Osage Nation on Christmas Day, 1889. After ensuring a liberal distribution of bribes, Emmet was acquitted and Bob released on bail, never to return to stand trial.

Emmet graduated from selling whiskey to Indians to horse stealing and by the summer of 1890 he and his brother Bob had garnered a formidable reputation as prolific horse-stealers.

Pursued by a local Posse, Emmet and Bob fled Kansas and resurfaced next in California. They went to live with their brother Bill who had a farm in the San Joaquin Valley.

The brothers soon had a fearsome reputation as wild

men, as they wore guns everywhere, which was uncommon in California at the time. They were soon joined by their brother Grat, again on the run from Kansas.

The brothers now decided to turn their hands to train robbery. Their first attempt was a monumental failure. On the evening of February 6, 1891 at Alila, Tulare County, California there was an attempted robbery of a Southern Pacific train by what would later be known as the first incarnation of the 'Dalton Gang'.

Emmet denied he was there, but what is known, is that his brothers Bob, Grat and Bill certainly were. So not wishing to label Emmet a liar, I would presume that Emmet was also present. His later denials were, in my view, an attempt to rehabilitate his rebellious youth.

While Bill kept any passengers from interfering by shooting over their heads, Bob and Grat forced the engineer to show them the location of the express car, which contained the safe and the money.

When the engineer tried to slip away, one of the brothers shot him in the stomach. Finding the express car on their own, Bob and Grat demanded that the guard inside open the heavy door. The guard refused and began firing down on them from a small spy hole. Thwarted, the brothers finally gave up and rode away empty-handed.

The engineer subsequently died and the attempted robbery was now a murder hunt.

Grat Dalton was arrested in Fresno on February 12 and a month later his brother Bill was apprehended and charged with harbouring Bob and Emmet.

It was only a matter of time before Emmet and Bob would be arrested, so they decided to leave California and fled to the Oklahoma Badlands.

At the subsequent trial Grat was found guilty, while Bill was acquitted and decided crime was not for him. He returned to life as a farmer.

Grat would later escape from jail and return to the family home near Coffeyville, where he would subsequently be joined by Bob and Emmet.

However, while in the Indian territories, Emmet was involved in a number of train robberies with Bob and associates, Charley Bryant and George Newcomb.

From May 1891 until July 1892, they robbed four trains.

At yet another later attempt at rehabilitation, Emmet would claim he played no part in these robberies but he was living with Bob in the Indian Territory at this time, so this claim is highly questionable.

Such was the notoriety of the Dalton Gang, that they were blamed for train robberies from California to Pennsylvania, but regardless of the speculation they were not guilty of these. This is because they were too busy robbing trains in Oklahoma and the Indian territories.

Again law enforcement officers began to close in on Emmet and he decided to return to his family in Kansas where he was reunited with Grat, and Bob would soon follow.

A period of relative calm in Emmet's life was soon to end, when Grat and Bob decided to carry out an audacious double bank robbery.

Emmet was recruited along with old Kansas friends Dick Broadwell and Bill Power.

The newly formed Dalton Gang decided to rob the First National and Condon banks, located across the street from each other in Coffeyville.

The raid was a pivotal moment in Emmet's life and

while so much has been written about it by others, I think it's best to recount the incident in his own words in an interview with the *Kansas City Star*, November 3, 1907:

Fully a month before the Coffeyville robbery Bob spoke of the large amount of money the banks there were supposed to have on deposit. We had lived there for a while. In fact I attended the public schools there. I was as well-known as any young-ster in the town.

Gradually Bob led up to the suggestion of rob-bing the banks at Coffeyville, mentioning that as I hadn't run before I probably would be game in this case. I discouraged the idea. The more I opposed, the more determined he seemed to be. I finally yielded. It was not so much that I wanted to turn outlaw, bandit and desperado as it was that I feared Bob would consider me lacking in nerve. In the gang as finally made up were five: Bob, my other brother Grattin, Bill Power, Dick Broadwell and myself.

"The night of October 4 we rode to a place about three miles out of Coffeyville and camped in a lit-tle draw that is from about 2 o'clock in the morn-ing until daylight, we lay upon our blankets on the ground. I didn't sleep much. I confess that I was nervous. The thought of the danger in the morrow's venture did not seem to occur to me as I remember it now. I believe I had sort of an idea that all there was to the matter was that we would merely ride into the town, rob the banks and ride away again. The fact of the matter is that I didn't take the affair with any degree of seriousness. I

was near Bob and that was about all there was in it.

"The next morning, October 5, 1892, this plan was outlined: We were to ride into town at shortly after 9 o'clock, dismount in an alley east of the Condon bank and the First National bank. These two banks were almost directly across the street from each other. Grat, Power and Broadwell were to enter Condon's bank while Bob and I crossed the street and rifled the First National. It was decided that we were to remain together after the robbery, make for a spot across the line in the Indian Territory. There we were to divide the money, separate and each man take care of himself.

"What a beautiful plan it was! All planned at daylight, but three hours later four of the planners were dead and the fifth, myself, was riddled with bullets. Can anyone imagine a more insane, crazier scheme? Here I was a kid of 19, known by practically everyone in the town; entering it without disguise or mask of any kind; making me a marked man forever; looked for as a wanderer fugitive, even if I had escaped. I think that my capture there was the best thing that could have happened. True, I have spent 15 years in prison, but these years instead of embittering me have taught me that to be square with your fellow man is the thing that wins out after all. I have also learned that when a fellow shows that he is trying to be on the square, even if he has been a convict, the average man is not going to give him a push, but rather a boost.

"We rode into Coffeyville shortly after 9 o'clock.

Bob and I went straight to the First National bank, while the other three went into the Condon's bank. In the First National were Thomas Ayres, the cashier, his son, the teller and bookkeeper and three customers. We drew our revolvers and threw them down on the crowd and told them to put up their hands. This they did. Bob walked behind the counter while I remained outside. He entered the vault, took all the currency in sight and took all the money on the counter, except some silver. This amounted to $23,000. He put it in a sack. We started to back out the way we had come, by the front door. Bob had handed me the sack. As Bob got to the front door a Winchester bullet buzzed close to his ear. He turned to me and said:

"Let's go by the back door.

"We left that way. We passed through the back yard of the bank into the alley, turned north to Eighth Street, as I remember the name now. On this we went west to another alley, then south to the alley where our horses were tied. The other three of the gang were not there."

Dalton drew a piece of paper toward him and made a rough sketch of the immediate surroundings of Coffeyville so far as they related to the fight.

"You can see by this," he continued, "the circuitous route we had to take to get back to our horses. When we got there it seemed that everybody in town had procured a Winchester and had opened fire. The moment we had ridden into town, most of the town was aroused. Many ran to the hardware store, which you will see is in a direct line with the alley. Still the other three didn't come. Just then a bullet struck me in the right shoulder. My right arm was put out of commission. My Winchester dropped from my right hand. Bob had begun to shoot.

"Right here I wish to make a statement. I didn't kill a soul that day, because I didn't fire a shot. I couldn't if I had wanted to. My right arm was as useless as if it hadn't been there.

"The shooting had now become general. It seemed that the bullets were coming from every house, store and fence within range of where we stood. We didn't mount."

"Bob said: 'The others are in trouble. Let's go and help them.' We didn't get a chance to start. They, at that moment came running out of the bank across the street, a running target for fifty or sixty guns, shooting as they ran. They joined us at the horses. I was trying to untie my horse with my left hand. Bob fell. I thought he was dead. Grat was the next. Then Bill Power went down. Broadwell managed to get on his horse and rode away down the street. He was found dead in the road a mile from town. Just as I was about to mount, a Winchester bullet struck me in the back, passed entirely through my body and came out. I got on my horse, nevertheless, and started. The money sack was on my saddle.

"As I turned the corner into the street, I looked back. Bob was sitting on the ground with his back to a large rock. I saw that he wasn't dead. I gave no thought to the consequences. I had one idea only. There was my brother alive and I might save him by carrying him away. No second thought of caution was needed. I wheeled my horse and went back into the firing. I learned afterward that fifteen men fired at me at once, but I wasn't scratched. I reached Bob's side, I leaned over and got hold of his wrist with my left hand, my right being useless. Bob was still alive. Just then a load of buckshot struck me in the back and the back of the neck. I remember that I said to Bob: 'My God, I'm killed!' Had I been sitting up straight the buckshot would have killed me. As it was they glanced off my back.

"That's the last I remember, for I rolled off my horse to the ground. I was in bed seventy-two days. I was advised to plead guilty to murder in the second degree and Judge Jerry McCune, now living and practicing law in Kansas City, sentenced me to the penitentiary for life."

"What delayed the three in the Condon's bank?" was asked.

"Oh yes, I had forgotten to tell you of that and by the way it was the real cause of the failure of the raid. When they went in, the bank vault was closed. The cashier told them the time lock was on".

"'How long will it be before it will be off?' asked Grat.

"'Three minutes,' was the answer.

"'We'll wait,' said Grat.

"At a time like that," said Emmet, "three minutes is a lifetime. It meant death to my two brothers and two companions and fifteen years in the penitentiary for me."

Source: Kansas City Star

It is also worth recounting that four citizens including a US marshal, Charles T Connelly, died defending the town.

A baying crowd wanted to lynch Emmet, but he was saved by a local, Dr Walter Wells, who assured the townspeople that Emmet would not survive his wounds. Wells then began to remove 23 bullets from Emmet's shattered and broken body.

The doctor provided ongoing medical treatment until October 11, when Emmett was taken to the local jail in Independence by County Sheriff John Callahan. Emmett recovered behind bars as he awaited trial under the charges of bank robbery and the murders of townspeople, George Cubine and Lucius Baldwin.

Emmet accepted he was guilty of bank robbery but fervently denied the charges of murder. He was adamant that he never fired a round during the raid and that he had killed no one. His firearms could not be checked, as they had been taken by souvenir hunters as he lay bleeding.

On Tuesday March 7, 1893, Emmet Dalton hobbled on crutches into the court room of Judge JD McCue, a Union Civil War veteran and former colleague and close friend of US marshal Charles T Connelly who had died in the bank raid. This did not bode well for an acquittal.

Emmet pleaded not guilty to murder but under pressure from his attorney FJ Fritch and his brother Bill, he pleaded guilty to second degree murder. He did so under the impression a deal could be made to avoid a life sentence and instead serve a sentence of up to 15 years.

However, Emmet had been lucky not to be lynched by the angry Coffeyville citizens and they were in no mood to accept a lenient sentence.

Much to Emmet's dismay, the Judge McCue did not accept a plea bargain and instead passed the harshest sentence available to him. Life imprisonment with hard labour.

Emmet, then only 23, was facing life behind bars in the Kansas state penitentiary. The only saving grace, was that his wounds prevented him from the arduous hard labour that many of his fellow inmates faced in the prison mine.

Emmet's prison time was uneventful and he was noted as a model prisoner. In July 1907, 14-and-a-half years since his incarceration, Emmet lobbied the Kansas Governor E W Hoch for parole on medical grounds.

Emmet had never really recovered from his wounds following the Coffeyville bank raid. His shoulder had been shattered and he needed an operation to save his right arm from amputation.

The Kansas penitentiary parole board asked the Governor to grant a temporary pardon so that Emmet could have his surgery in Kansas City. This was granted and the Governor was so taken with Emmet's good behaviour that he arranged for the parole board to grant an unconditional pardon and end his time in prison.

As he gave the pardon to Emmet the Governor told him:

"I do not believe that good government will suffer because of the fact you are a free man."

Now on November 2, 1907, at the age of 37, Emmet Dalton faced up to his new life as a free man.

Emmett Dalton soon proved himself a useful citizen. He went into business with his cousin in Tulsa, opened a tailor shop, and joined the Tulsa "boosters", a group of business men who wanted to market the area. He would later accompany them on a promotional trip to Washington DC.

In Washington he went to the White House and, with the other businessmen from Tulsa, met President Roosevelt.

Emmet also had someone to share his new found freedom with, when he married Mrs Julia Lewis on September 1, 1908.

Julia was the widow of a well-known train robber and sometime associate in Emmet's youth, Earnest Lewis, who died in a bloody fight with United States Marshals Keeler and Williams in Kansas City in November 1907.

Lewis had killed Marshall Williams during the battle, in which more than 20 shots were fired in a small room filled with smoke.

Emmet had known Julia Lewis for twenty years and first met her when working as a cowboy.

She was the daughter of 'Texas Johnson' and lived with her parents near the Kansas line, 18 miles north of Bartlesville. She and Dalton were about the same age, and they rode races, practiced shooting with rifles and rode their ponies to all of the dances within 30 miles of the Johnson home.

Emmet and Julia lost touch when he fled to California, but began a brief romance when he returned home prior to the Coffeyville bank raids. She was pregnant with another man's child, but this did not deter Emmet.

However, all romance ended abruptly when Emmet was sentenced to life in Kansas state penitentiary.

Julia kept in touch over the years, writing to him and spent a great deal of her time working with his mother to gain him a pardon. She even visited those who opposed the pardon and persuaded them to give Emmett another trial. She did more than all others to wear out the opposition to Emmet's pardon.

Ever since his release from prison he had become dismayed at the inaccurate and in some cases outrageous tales in the papers and popular western magazines about the Dalton Gang and their exploits. He decided to set the record straight and in 1918, he published his first book, *Beyond The Law*.

He now moved to Hollywood to make a movie version of the book where Emmet played himself.

He used the film to tour the country and lecture against crime. Emmett Dalton was determined that other young men would not follow in his path. He used the Coffeyville bank raid as a moral lesson for the youth of America.

Emmett began a short-lived acting career and starred in several short films based on events from his life, *When a Man's a Pal*, *Across the Chasm*, *Showdown Jim* and *The Man of the Desert*.

These were not successful and Emmet's acting career came to an end but ever resourceful and now settled in Hollywood, Emmet turned his attention to real estate and construction. Hollywood was expanding quickly and demand for new homes was high.

In 1929 Emmet and Julia returned to Coffeyville to place a headstone on the graves of his brothers who had fallen during the infamous bank raid.

In 1931 he wrote another book, *When the Daltons Rode*, which would later be turned into another movie, starring Randolph Scott in 1940.

A year later, after being diagnosed with diabetes,

Emmet's health began to fade and he retired from the construction business and concentrated more on writing stories for Western magazines. His health rapidly declined and he suffered a number of strokes.

On July 4, 1937, Emmett suffered a final stroke. He passed away quietly on July 13, with Julia by his side.

Emmet Dalton was undoubtedly a criminal for a period of his life but his incarceration certainly reformed him and he devoted his life to ensuring others would not repeat his mistakes. I will leave you with one of his most famous quotes.

> *"As I once had a life sentence, and from my experience for observation along these lines, I have become unalterably opposed to capital punishment. The aim of society should never be to hurt, but to cure."*

Wise words from the Hollywood outlaw.

8

Big Jim O'Leary
The Gangster Whose Family Rose From The Ashes

ONE of the most successful Irish-American crime bosses in the history of Chicago was James Patrick O'Leary, whose criminal career rose from the ashes of the Great Chicago fire of October 1871.

James O'Leary was born to Irish immigrants Patrick and Catherine O'Leary on January 23, 1869 in their home at 137 DeKoven Street in Chicago. It was at this address, that the Great Fire of Chicago started two years later, an event that would shape the lives and destiny of the entire O'Leary family.

Chicago in 1871 was growing rapidly and was a warren of streets and side alleys of wooden buildings.

October of that year was unseasonably dry and on the night of October 8, a fire began in a barn at the O'Leary family home. A high wind and the dry conditions created a firestorm that destroyed thousands of buildings, killed over 300 people and caused $200 million in damages.

In the aftermath of the devastation, the *Chicago Tribune* was quick to attribute blame. One of its reporters, Michael Ahern, published a story which claimed that the great fire had been started by a cow kicking over a lantern while it was being milked. Ahern did not name the owner of the cow, but as the fire had started in the O'Leary's barn, Catherine O'Leary was soon everyone's chief suspect.

The local newspapers began printing caricatures of Catherine milking the cow and starting the fire.

Soon publications all over the United States followed suit and the blame for the destruction was now lying firmly at the feet of Catherine O'Leary.

At the official inquiry into the disaster, Catherine fervently denied being at fault. She testified under oath that she had been asleep in bed when the fire had started and was unaware of the danger.

This was reinforced by the testimony of the first person to raise the alarm, a man with an unusual name, Daniel 'Peg Leg' Sullivan.

Peg Leg was a neighbour of the O'Learys and he testified that he had gone to visit them at around 6pm and that while he talked to Mr O'Leary, his wife was absent, asleep in bed.

He left the O'Leary house at around 8pm. On his way home he paused to light his pipe on the corner of the O'Learys' property and it was then he first spotted the flames coming from their barn. Despite having only one leg, he claimed to have run to help, shouting fire!

He reached the barn and freed the animals inside and then roused the O'Learys, who he claimed were still unaware of the fire.

However, the *Chicago Tribune* story and anti-Irish sentiment, still strong at the time, made scapegoats of Catherine O'Leary and her family.

Even more outrageous stories soon circulated. One claimed she was drunk at the time of the fire and had hidden the evidence of her crime. Others stated that all the incriminating evidence had been hidden to protect the O'Learys.

The official report from the inquiry did not blame Catherine O'Leary, simply saying:

"Whether it originated from a spark blown from a chimney on that windy night, or was set on fire by human agency, we are unable to determine."

However, the idea that the O'Leary's cow had started the fire caught the popular imagination, further stimulated by Ahern's *Chicago Tribune* article.

Michael Ahern would later admit in 1893 that he had made the whole story up. However, it was too late for the O'Learys whose reputation had been tarnished and finances ruined.

They were forced to move with the infant James and his two siblings to a south side Chicago slum where James would grow up haunted by the stigma of the false allegations against his family.

It was in these rough streets that James grew up watching his mother gradually die heartbroken from acute pneumonia on July 3, 1895. James was determined that he would drag himself up from this poverty and unwanted notoriety.

Leaving school early, James was nevertheless a very intelligent young man and he soon started working for local bookmakers. He decided to strike out on his own and set up his own bookmaking business based out of Long Beach Indiana, which was an off-track betting resort.

This venture didn't last long and he soon went bankrupt and was forced to work as a meat packer in the Union Stockyards to make ends meet. It was while working there he was given the nickname that would stay with him for the rest of his life, Big Jim.

O'Leary married Annie McLaughlin, whose family lived next to the O'Learys at the time of the fire. They were the parents of two sons and three daughters.

Ever the entrepreneur and determined to make something of himself, Big Jim O'Leary left the stockyards in 1892 and opened a saloon bar which included Turkish baths, a restaurant, a billiards room, and a bowling alley.

Going back to his bookmaker roots, he also posted detailed race track results and other betting information near the entrance to the Stock Yards, which proved highly lucrative.

As his empire began to grow, O'Leary expanded further, opening a pool hall and another bookmakers in the rear of his saloon.

He quickly became one of the leading bookmakers in Chicago and was known for taking bets on everything from Presidential candidates to changes in the weather.

O'Leary had a reputation for fair dealing. Chicago's longtime alderman-vice lord, Michael 'Hinky Dink' Kenna, said of him:

> "He was a square shooter. Big Jim never welshed on a bet. He was a good loser and his patrons had confidence in him that he would always pay off if he lost."

O'Leary refused to bribe police, instead he had his business fortified including the construction of iron and zinc-layered oak entrance doors to his bar, which were, according to Jim himself: "Fire proof, bomb-proof, and police-proof."

Jim became tired of constant police harassment and requests for bribes and decided to try something novel. He bought a steamship, The City of Traverse, and began to run an illegal gambling operation on Lake Michigan.

Frequently raided by the police the venture only lasted until 1907.

O'Leary was continually under surveillance by the authorities and under attack from rival gambling gangs.

However, Big Jim was always one step ahead of them all and though he was indicted a number of times for gambling, he was only ever convicted once in 25 years. And as it was a first offence at the age of 53, he was fined only $100.

Perhaps one reason that Big Jim evaded conviction for so long, was the fact his son James Jr was married to the daughter of Chicago's chief of police. O'Leary also had a network of informers and was usually tipped off about any police raid.

One year before his river boat venture failed in 1906, Mayor Edward Fitzsimmons Dunne briefly revoked O'Leary's saloon license.

Again Big Jim was, as the Irish say, 'too cute' for them. He arranged to 'sell' his Saloon to a trusted employee who then reapplied for a license.

Once this was granted, Big Jim was back in business.

The authorities were not the only problem Big Jim faced. During 1907 and into 1908, a war erupted between the gambling factions in Chicago. O'Leary's Saloon was bombed in 1907 and twice in 1908 but undeterred Big

Jim rebuilt every time and meted out bloody retribution in return. The war ended with the death of Chicago crime lord, Michael Cassius MacDonald.

The path was now clear for Big Jim to take complete control over the gambling on Chicago's southwest side around his old stomping ground of the Union Stock yards. He duly did so, also branching out into supplying illegal whiskey during Prohibition.

No man who reached such heights could do so without ruthlessness and, despite his genial appearance, Big Jim was capable of violence.

He was strongly suspected of involvement in one of the most infamous murders in Chicago criminal history, the death of Italian mob boss, James Colosimo.

Colosimo immigrated to Chicago from Italy in 1895. Starting as a barman, he cleverly cultivated connections with the police and corrupt politicians to quickly rise through the ranks of the Italian crime gangs.

As his power and wealth grew, the flamboyant Colosimo acquired a nickname, 'Diamond Jim'. This was because of his habit of wearing white suits and diamond pins.

He had two passions — women and money. In 1902, Colosimo married Victoria Moresco, an established Chicago Madame, and the pair began to open a series of brothels. Within a few years, Colosimo controlled 200 brothels, using the profits to expand into gambling and the protection rackets.

By 1909, Colosimo's success was under threat from the other gangs in Chicago and he realised he needed extra muscle. He recruited Johnny 'The Fox' Torrio from Brooklyn and made him his second in command.

The following year, Colosimo opened a self-named restaurant, Colosimo's Cafe, at 2126 South Wabash, in Chicago.

In 1919, Torrio brought his old Brooklyn lieutenant, Al Capone, to work in Chicago as a bartender and bouncer, providing Capone his introduction to Chicago. Capone had left Brooklyn after threats to his life from the Irish White Hand gang.

When Prohibition went into effect in 1920, Torrio pushed for the gang to enter into bootlegging, but Colosimo refused as he felt prostitution was easier and safer. Torrio decided that if he was to reap the massive rewards of Prohibition, then a change of leadership was necessary.

In May 1920, Colosimo went out of town to marry his second wife, Dale Winter, after he had deserted his first wife Victoria.

On his return a week later, he was informed by Torrio that a delivery of bootleg whiskey from O'Leary would be arriving at his club.

When Colosimo appeared at the club to wait for its delivery, he was shot and killed. The initial murder suspect was his new wife Dale, infuriated by his infidelity after just one week of marriage, but no one was ever arrested for the murder.

Big Jim was a serious suspect for two reasons. Firstly O'Leary was delivering whiskey on a regular basis and would not be suspected by Colosimo. Secondly, and more importantly, he wished to create an alliance with the rising man in the Italian Mafia, Johnny Torrio, and what better way to do that than to help eliminate the obstacle to Torrio's rise to the top.

Late in life, O'Leary mused to a reporter about his success:

> *"How much have I cleaned up? I'm satisfied with the results. I've got enough to take a trip around the world when I sell my shop. Then I'm going to settle down in some little town."*

Big Jim never got to do that, as he died of natural causes at the age of 56 in his home at 726 West Garfield Boulevard, on January 23, 1925. When Jim died his entire estate was valued at just $10,200, despite having made millions of dollars over the years. But Big Jim O'Leary knew you had to keep up a good front and he always wanted to show his family had risen from the ashes of the great fire.

Jim and his wife are buried next to his parents in a Chicago cemetery.

After his death, the O'Leary gambling house continued to be run by a business partner for a few years until, somewhat ironically, the place burned down in the second-biggest fire in Chicago history, the 1934 Stockyards fire.

Today, the Chicago Fire Department training academy is located on the site of the O'Leary property where the Great Chicago Fire started.

In 1997, the Chicago City Council passed a resolution exonerating Catherine O'Leary, an Irish immigrant who died in 1895, and her cow.

I'm sure Big Jim would have been pleased his family was finally cleared.

9

Vincent 'Mad Dog' Coll
The Child Killer

VINCENT COLL was born on July 20, 1908 in the Irish speaking parish of Gweedore which, at the time, was a beautiful but impoverished region of County Donegal.

Gweedore was rich in beauty but lacking in opportunities and employment and its biggest industry in 1908 was emigration.

When Vincent was less than a year old, his parents decided to do what many Irish people did in those days, they emigrated to America to seek a better life.

With their seven children, the Colls settled in the Irish enclave of the Bronx, but found that their lives in New York were not much better than the one that they had left behind in Ireland.

They still lived in dire poverty, leading Coll's father to eventually desert the family. Coll's mother and all but one of his six siblings died before he turned 12 years old.

After his mother died, Coll and his brother Peter were placed in a number of Catholic orphanages, but were found to be uncontrollable by the clergy who ran these institutions.

Eventually the Coll brothers were sent to live with an aunt named Mary Friel, another native of Gweedore.

If the authorities thought that living with a close relative would turn the boys into law-abiding citizens, they were badly mistaken. The brothers used the Friel home as a base from which they organised a juvenile street gang made up mainly of Italian youths who had dreams of becoming top Mafioso, like the leading Italian gangsters who were beginning to make a name for themselves in New York City.

Vincent was a difficult child, constantly in trouble and he was expelled from several local Catholic schools before he even reached his teens. On the streets he had swapped formal education for another form of learning — that of the art of crime, with a local gang called the Gophers, led by Owen 'Owney' Madden.

While school books had been no attraction, Coll was a fast learner in the art of crime and he soon came to the attention of the established gangster, Dutch Schultz.

Shultz was a Jewish-American mob leader who had amassed power and wealth through bootlegging and the numbers racket.

In the violent poverty-stricken era of 1920s New York, Coll was not afraid to do whatever it took to rise to the top of the gangster tree. His aggressive and volatile personality made him a man to be feared and his willingness to murder to get what he wanted made him a trusted lieutenant of Schultz. He soon became one of the Prohibition era's most feared enforcers. He had no qualms about using violence and was a ruthless killer.

As the body count rose, the authorities started to take a keen interest in Coll.

In 1927, at just 19, Vincent Coll was accused of the murder of a speakeasy owner who had refused to sell bootleg alcohol for Dutch Schultz.

Coll was found not guilty and acquitted, which was no surprise as Schultz used his influence to tamper with the jury. It was a matter of 'find Coll innocent or else'. Vincent walked free and the jury avoided harm.

Clearly guilty, Vincent showed no remorse; in fact he now felt invincible and was soon out of control. He believed that money and intimidation made gangsters like him untouchable.

Seeking money to fund his increasingly extravagant lifestyle, Coll became freelance and robbed the Sheffield Farms dairy in the Bronx of $17,000 without Schultz's authorisation or permission.

When the two men next met, Schultz reminded Coll he could only operate with his approval.

Coll told Schultz that it was his methods that had helped build his empire and rather than apologise, he demanded to be made his partner. Shultz refused and a rift developed between the men who had once been close friends.

While Coll was a violent man, Shultz was on a different level of viciousness and not a man to be crossed. Vincent had made a strategic error, and a paranoid and ruthless enemy.

Coll was now a marked and isolated figure and the final break with Schultz came in January 1931. Vincent was arrested and despite their animosity, Schultz put up the bail money. This was a surprising but clever move. Shultz did not want Vincent giving the authorities any information on his activities and despite his loathing for Coll he'd rather pay up than have him behind bars.

Vincent did not attend his trial which meant the bail money was forfeited. Shultz demanded Coll pay him back but Vincent refused. This was the final breakdown in an already fractious relationship and the two men went to war.

Coll left the Shultz operation and proceeded to take a dozen members of the Schultz gang to join him in this new criminal enterprise. Coll's new gang and Schultz's mob engaged in a bloody battle.

To finance his war against Shultz, Coll's gang began to kidnap rival gangsters and hold them for ransom. This was a sideline Coll found highly lucrative and he was very good at it.

As the war dragged on Shultz was terrified by the savagery of Coll's attack on his organisation. He felt Coll was reckless and his destructive nature was bad for business.

Coll was determined to drive Shultz out of New York. He began by hijacking Schultz's beer trucks and would then sell the beer at discounted rates to bar owners. What did he care, it was all profit to him.

He then burned down a warehouse belonging to Shultz, destroying a vast quantity of bootleg beer.

Coll cranked up the violence and he and his gang assassinated several of Shultz's closest associates and even tried unsuccessfully to murder Schultz.

Vincent had to be stopped and Dutch Shultz retaliated in May 1931 when he arranged for the murder of Vincent's brother Peter.

Coll's tactics so terrified Schultz that he also offered a large sum of money to several policemen to murder Coll. Such was Vincent's reputation that they turned down the offer.

Even the police were now afraid of Vincent.

Distraught at the murder of his brother Peter, Coll responded with a maelstrom of violence in the following three weeks he personally murdered four of Schultz's men. Despite the rising body count the war was a stalemate and finally petered out into an uneasy truce, but both men would not forget or forgive. It was peace, but only for now.

Despite the stalemate, Vincent Coll did manage to bully his way into the control of some sections of Harlem and the Bronx that were previously controlled by Shultz.

He soon owned a number of bars, not by purchasing them but by telling the previous owners they would be killed if they did not leave New York. Given Vincent's reputation and track record, most left.

Vincent was fast becoming a major player in the New York criminal landscape.

However, he was also becoming an inconvenience for the New York criminal fraternity. Violence was part of everyday life but only if it was good for business and, for many, Vincent was bad for profits.

Coll also had no friends in the underworld due to his ongoing lucrative sideline of kidnapping other gangsters and holding them for ransom.

Whilst undoubtedly psychotic, Coll was no fool. He knew his victims would not report their kidnappings because of the underworld's code of silence. Also any freed gangster would have a hard time explaining to the police authorities or the tax man where the ransom money that they paid had come from.

It wasn't just gangsters he kidnapped; Vincent and his gang began to diversify and started to kidnap showbusiness stars and successful businessmen. They began with showbusiness legend, Rudy Vallée, and he received $100,000 for the singer's release. Next to be taken was Sherman Billingsly, owner of the Stork Club, the most famous restaurant in New York, whose family paid Coll $25,000 for his release.

Then Billy Warren, a New York banker, parted with $83,000 to gain his freedom.

Coll then had the nerve to kidnap George De Mange, a close aide to Irish mob boss and his old friend Owney Madden and forced Madden to pay $38,500 for his release. This was a grave insult to his fellow Irish mobster and one he would eventually avenge.

There were many other kidnappings that received no publicity, but all of them added to the growing wealth of Coll, who was making more money from this activity than he made in his war with Shultz.

But this enterprise was not generating any publicity for the gang in the newspapers. Coll was a vain man who craved the notoriety of Owney Madden and Dutch Shultz. He was frustrated that his terror tactics were not making him a superstar in the New York night clubs.

What Vincent failed to realise was that his fellow mobsters would pay journalists to promote them in a positive light. Coll's criminal activities, whilst newsworthy, didn't generate any feelings of respect or adulation.

This is not to say that Vincent didn't try to develop his image as a gangster; he was intelligent and handsome and spent a fortune on suits and hats.

However, he and his gang were so feared for their brutality that no matter how well they dressed, everyone thought of them as common criminals. When he visited the famous clubs of New York he desperately wanted the kind of respect that Owney Madden received, or that given to leading mafia mobsters like Lucky Luciano.

However, it was obvious to him that the club owners reacted with fear, not respect. He knew they saw him as a vicious young thug who was extremely dangerous or who might even kidnap them.

Overall, Coll wanted respect from his fellow Irishmen, but this was not forthcoming. He was once deeply humiliated at an Irish fundraiser in Brooklyn.

A dance had been organised by fellow Donegal immigrants for a Gweedore family who had lost everything in a recent fire.

Vincent went along with his girlfriend and future fiancée, Lottie Kreisberger. They entered the dance hall in designer clothes, looking every inch the successful couple. And they wanted everyone to know about it.

Vincent had lost touch with many other Donegal immigrants as his criminal career took off and this was the first time many of them had seen this infamous gangster. They didn't hold him in awe but in fear. Vincent may have thought he was a celebrity but to these Irish men and women trying to make a living in America, he was nothing but a violent and notorious killer.

Vincent was taken aback by their reaction to him, no one approached him to give him a friendly greeting and everyone he talked to was aloof and did not hide their fear and distrust. It was plain Vincent was not welcome, even amongst his own people.

There were several of Coll's second cousins present and they were so embarrassed by his presence that they left the venue without identifying themselves.

Vincent was shocked and hurt. He had seen how the Irish respected Owney Madden and his gang and for the first time it was clear to him that he was not respected in the Irish community in New York.

Despite all his wealth, designer clothes and beautiful girlfriend, it was clear that his fellow Donegal immigrants despised him. The Gweedore immigrants had a reason for their attitude. These people had left Ireland to escape poverty, they had journeyed across the Atlantic to America to try and find a better life for them and their children. Through hard work many of them were already sending their children to college and some had bought their own homes. They wanted to make America their home and believed that law and order was essential for them to do so.

The brutal lifestyle of Coll and his gang was, to them, a menace to decent people and a threat to the integration of the Irish into American society.

Many were also embarrassed and angry that the press had labelled Coll as the 'Gangster from Gweedore'. This they viewed as an insult to not only them, but their parish back in Ireland.

That night highlighted to Coll he was not welcome among the Donegal Irish and he would limit his contact with them going forward.

A hurt and embarrassed Coll would put a different spin on his visit to Brooklyn when he talked about it later. He described the Gweedore people as:

"Little nobodies who were jealous of his success."

He also stated that they lacked ambition and were willing to settle for little weekly salaries instead of reaching for the stars as he had. He also said they were cowards who were afraid of the police.

Perhaps still angry from this perceived slight, Vincent restarted the war with Dutch Shultz. On July 28, 1931, Coll attempted to kidnap Joey Rao, a major Schultz lieutenant.

The attempt failed and in the ongoing gun battle on a public street, a five-year-old child, Michael Vengalli, was killed and several other children wounded.

The enraged media, shocked by the brutality of the incident, dubbed Coll a "baby killer" and filled the pages of the newspapers every day with negative coverage of him. The media called him the worst criminal in America, and the FBI named him as #1 on its famed 'Ten Most Wanted List'.

New York Mayor Jimmy Walker, the son of an Irish immigrant, christened Coll a 'Mad Dog' and the nickname made for great headlines and it stuck to this very day.

While on the run, the newly christened 'Mad Dog Coll' approached another notorious Irish gangster, Legs Diamond, and tried to form an alliance with him.

Perhaps fearing the noose was tightening around him in New York, he proposed a joint venture with Diamond to smuggle beer and whiskey into other states far from New York City.

Coll told Diamond they could make a fortune. Diamond was cautious in his dealings with Coll and he had every reason to be since he knew Coll had once accepted a Mafia contract to assassinate him.

However, before the new partnership could be created, New York State police captured most of the Coll gang, and a few days later Coll himself and Legs Diamond were captured and Vincent was charged with capital murder of the five-year old boy in New York.

The general consensus was that Coll would be found guilty and sentenced to death. The press speculated that Mad Dog Coll had an urgent appointment with the electric chair.

Mayor Walker, ever conscious of public opinion, was making it clear he wanted a quick trial, a guilty verdict and an execution to quell the massive public anger at Vincent.

However, this was not to be because Coll was acquitted in a bizarre trial.

Vincent's lawyer was the famous defense attorney, Samuel Leibowitz, much used by the gangster fraternity and for good reason.

Leibowitz was the most successful criminal lawyer of his generation and the go-to man whenever a major criminal figure needed a defense attorney.

He was a frustrated actor and the court room became his stage where his oratorical skills and flair for the dramatic made him a formidable opponent for any prosecutor. Despite his showmanship, the real reason for Leibowitz's successful track record was his preparation — he left nothing to chance.

Throughout the 1920s Leibowitz defended a who's who of criminal history and usually got them off.

During the trial Leibowitz used every trick in his formidable arsenal to select a jury he felt was as sympathetic as possible to Vincent.

The turning point in the trial was focused on the key prosecution witness George Brecht. Leibowitz managed to destroy his credibility and that of the prosecution's, when it was revealed that Brecht made a covert living as a witness at criminal trials.

The trial was now a farce and the court room descended into uproar at this revelation. The prosecution case had collapsed and the Judge was left with no choice but to allow Coll to walk free in December 1931.

Despite the let-off, Vincent did not learn his lesson. Even while awaiting trial, he embarked on what would be his final fatal mistake, the attempted murder of Charles 'Lucky' Luciano, one of the most powerful gangsters in America.

During the trial Vincent was hired by the New York 'Godfather', Salvatore Maranzano, who despite being the most powerful mobster in the city, feared Luciano would kill him and take over. It seems paranoia was not just restricted to Dutch Schultz.

Despite the risks, Coll readily agreed to murder Luciano for $50,000, the highest amount yet offered for a single mob murder.

On September 10, 1931, Maranzano invited Luciano to a meeting at his office to discuss re-drawing the mob map of New York. The real plan was for Coll to arrive later and kill Luciano during the meeting.

Luciano, who had a wide network of informers, had learned of the plot against him and decided to act first. He sent his own men, who killed Maranzano before Coll turned up.

While Luciano knew his life was in danger he did not know the identity of the man Maranzano hired to kill him.

The fleeing assassins saw Coll arriving and informed Luciano that he must be the intended hitman, and this sealed Vincent's fate.

An enraged Luciano, while flattered at the high level

of the bounty on his head, arranged for Coll's old friend from the Gophers, Owney Madden, now boss of the Irish criminal syndicate in Hell's Kitchen, to place a similar $50,000 bounty on Vincent Coll's head.

Two violent hitmen, Leonard Scarnici and Anthony Fabrizzo, accepted Madden's bounty and the hunt for Coll began.

Vincent was again in hiding but, acting on a tip-off, Scarnici and Fabrizzo burst into a Bronx apartment where they believed Coll was sleeping. They found six people there. Not knowing Vincent Coll by sight they decided it was better to be safe than sorry and decided to shoot everyone anyway. In the ensuing bloodbath, three people died and three hung to life; but Vincent Coll was not amongst them.

Vincent was delayed elsewhere and arrived at the apartment after the shooting. The carnage was brutal and the shocked New York authorities informed the mob that this bloodshed had to end.

Dutch Shultz and Madden also decided to act; this, after all, was getting bad for business.

A few days later, Coll received word that Madden, whom he trusted from his Gopher days, wanted to speak with him. Coll was informed Madden had worked out a settlement between all the gangs that would make everyone happy and save his life. Vincent had known Madden all his life and trusted him, but this was to prove a fatal mistake.

A meeting was arranged in Hell's Kitchen where he would be safe because the neighbourhood was under Madden's protection.

To avoid any further mistakes and to ensure Coll

would now be recognised by his assassins, Dutch Schultz arranged for an old Coll associate, Abraham 'Bo' Weinberg, to work with the hitmen, Scarnici and Fabrizzo. Weinberg and Coll had worked together under Schultz but Weinberg had stayed loyal to Shultz during the ensuing war between the men.

Vincent was now a desperate man. He was being hunted by every mob hitman in New York, all wanting the $50k bounty Luciano had placed on his head. On February 7, 1932, Vincent checked into the Cornish Arms Hotel on 23rd Street.

The next day Coll entered the phone booth in the London Chemists drug store at 314 West 23rd Street at Eighth Avenue. He had been told by Owney Madden the previous day to call him to discuss the truce. Madden had set him up and Vincent had walked right into an ambush.

Weinberg identified Coll to the hitmen waiting in a car as Coll walked by and Scarnici and Fabrizzo stepped out to murder Vincent.

Only one assassin, Scarnici, entered the drug store, Fabrizzo and Weinberg waited on the sidewalk. Police reports later detailed that, as Scarnici passed cashier George Scott, who was waiting on a customer, a Dr Leo Katz, he turned to Scott and quietly said, "Keep cool now."

Scarnici had a submachine gun hidden under his overcoat and as he approached the phone booth he drew this and fired two bursts into Coll as he talked to Madden.

Taking no chances, Scarnici checked Coll was dead, then calmly replaced the gun under his coat and turned to walk out of the drug store. Passing the two witnesses Scott and Katz, he turned to them and raised a finger to his lips and made a 'Shhh' motion.

He left the store and re-joined Weinberg and Fabrizzo and all three sped off into Eighth Avenue traffic. The hit on Vincent Coll had lasted less than 90 seconds.

The Coroner's report revealed that while a total of 15 bullets were removed from Coll's body at the morgue, it appeared that many more may have passed through him. The *New York Evening Post* reported:

> *"How many shots were fired is not known. Some witnesses said fifteen others said fifty. As the killer backed out of the store, the door of the booth opened slowly and Coll's body pitched forward, three bullets in the head, three in the chest, and one in the abdomen and eight and the arms and legs."*

Vincent 'Mad Dog' Coll's killers were never definitely identified. Dutch Schultz's attorney, Dixie Davis, later claimed that gangster, Bo Weinberg, was the getaway driver of the limousine. Another suspect was one of Coll's own men, Edward Popke aka Fats McCarthy.

The submachine gun that killed Coll was found a year later in the possession of a Hell's Kitchen gunman named 'Tough' Tommy Protheroe, who used it during a 1933 saloon killing.

On May 16, 1935, Protheroe and his girlfriend Elizabeth Connors were shot and killed by unknown gunmen in Queens. Was this in revenge for Vincent?

What we do know is that no one was ever arrested for Vincent Coll's death.

Despite a love of glamour, fashion and a deep rooted

need to be respected, Vincent was mourned only by Lottie Coll who, despite taking Vincent's name, was never officially married to Coll.

They had applied for a marriage license in New York City in January 1932 but Vincent's death less than a month later ended their marriage hopes. However, the press would always refer to her as the wife of Mad Dog Coll.

Vincent was buried in St Raymond's cemetery in the Bronx. Dutch Schultz himself sent a wreath to Coll's funeral bearing a banner with the message, "From the boys".

As is normally the case, all three of the men involved in Vincent's death also met brutal ends.

Fabrizzo was murdered on November 20, 1932 after a botched attempt on the life of Bugsy Siegel.

The gunman, Scarnici, was executed in the electric chair in Sing Sing prison for the 1933 murder of a police detective.

Bo Weinberg didn't receive much gratitude from Dutch Shultz for his part in the demise of Vincent Coll. Shultz arranged for him to disappear after discovering he was in league with Lucky Luciano to have him killed.

Dutch Shultz continued to operate his rackets for only a few more years. On October 23, 1935, he was killed at the Palace Chophouse in Newark, New Jersey, on orders from the new National Crime Syndicate headed by none other than Lucky Luciano.

As for Owney Madden, well, he left New York shortly after the death of Vincent Coll and his story is one we shall hear more of in Chapter 12.

So ended the violent and notorious life of Vincent

'Mad Dog' Coll at the age of just 23 years. The story of Coll lives on and in 1961, the movie *Mad Dog Coll* was released, staring John Chandler as Coll, with up-and-coming actors, Telly Savalas and Gene Hackman in minor roles.

10

Richard 'Peg Leg' Lonergan
The Man Even Al Capone Feared

I N the criminal fraternity many underworld figures are known by nicknames and one of the most memorable in the Irish-American gangster lexicon has to be that of Richard 'Peg Leg' Lonergan, who was one of the leaders of the New York Irish criminal group, The White Hand Gang.

Richard Lonergan came into the world on January 16, 1900. He was one of 15 children born to Irish immigrants Mary and John Lonergan. Nothing much is known about his siblings other than that one sister, Anna Lonergan, would became known as 'Queen of the Irishtown Docks' and would later marry his close friend and fellow gang member, Bill Lovett.

Richard was raised in Irish Town, an impoverished Irish-American enclave between the Manhattan and Brooklyn waterfront.

His early life was traumatic and he did not enjoy a happy childhood. His father, a noted bare-knuckle boxer, was a member of the Jay Street Gang and a gambler. Also a heavy drinker he regularly abused his wife and children.

When Richard was just 13, his mother Mary was charged with the murder of his father. John Lonergan attacked his wife in a drunken rage and drew a gun intending to murder his wife. Mary fought back and in the ensuing struggle, the gun went off and John Lonergan lay dead. Mary stood trial for murder, but gave a plea of self-defence and was acquitted by the judge.

It was in this maelstrom of poverty and abuse that Richard Lonergan himself turned to crime, joining local street gangs and taking to robbing passengers on rail cars and trolley trams.

It was during one such robbery that he escaped an early death. Fleeing the scene of the crime, he fell under a trolley car and lost his right leg. His injury meant he received not only a prosthetic leg but a lifelong nickname, 'Peg Leg'.

Despite this, Lonergan still earned a fearsome reputation in Irish Town and on the Brooklyn waterfront as a tough street fighter. However, while vicious in nature he was also an intelligent and a shrewd businessman.

He once received a bicycle but couldn't use it because of his leg. He started to rent his bike to others in his neighbourhood and with the money he earned, he bought a couple of new bikes. He eventually started a bike shop where he sold and rented bikes.

Even as a young man, his hatred of Italian-Americans was well known. This stemmed from an incident at his bike shop when a Sicilian gangster approached him to sell drugs.

While not adverse to the drug trade, Lonergan refused as this would insult fellow Irish gangsters and he viciously beat the man.

The Italian wasn't too pleased with this response and he used Mafia police connections to close Lonergan down, on the excuse that he was selling stolen merchandise.

Lonergan lost his store and had to work on a farm. There, his hatred of Italians simmered and he met and befriended Bill Lovett which would change his life forever.

Richard introduced his new-found friend to his sister Anna and she and Bill were soon married.

Both Richard and Bill became members of the Irish White Hand Gang under the leadership of Dinny Meehan.

The White Hand Gang was one of the most famous Irish-American gangs with a short but bloody history.

The White Hand Gang was the coming together of a number of existing Irish-American gangs such as the Frankie Byrne Gang, Jay Street Gang and the Red Onion Gang.

They organised themselves to benefit from the lucrative waterfront rackets and to resist the growing influence of the Sicilian Black Hand Italian mafia, who enviously coveted the wealth that could be made along the New York and Brooklyn shoreline.

The driving force behind the creation of the White Hand gang was Dinny Meehan, a folk hero in the slums of Brooklyn.

From 1900 until 1925, a continuous war raged between The White Hand Gang and the Italian mob along the New York waterfront.

The White Handers retained a firm grip on the Brooklyn Bridge to Red Hook sections and collected tribute from barge and wharf owners.

Those who declined to pay saw their wharves and vessels looted, burned or wrecked. All longshoremen had to pay a daily commission for the right to work. Some paid willingly because they were Irish and saw their salvation in the vows of the White Handers to keep the docks clear of Italians.

Ruling with a grip of iron, The White Hand Gang drove the Italian Mafia from the New York waterfront. Such was the viciousness that the Italian Mafia decided to send one of its rising stars, a certain Al Capone to Chicago to ensure his safety, when they found out he was on the White Handers' death list.

However, as we shall see, his relationship with The White Hand Gang would not end there.

'Peg Leg' Lonergan rose quickly through The White Hand Gang, becoming its Number 3, chiefly due to his vicious reputation and the fact his brother-in-law who now had the nickname 'Wild' Bill Lovett, was now the Number 2 to Dinny Meehan.

Dinny Meehan, whilst only 23, was old school and concentrated on collecting tribute from ship captains and factory bosses.

Peg Leg and Wild Bill saw great potential in prohibition and urged the White Hand gang to expand into this lucrative market. Meehan disagreed and a feud began to simmer between the men which boiled over into violence.

On the evening of March 31, 1920, Dinny Meehan was shot multiple times while in bed with his wife Sadie (who was wounded in the shoulder). No one was charged for Meehan's murder, but everyone knew it was ordered by Richard Lonergan and Wild Bill Lovett.

For the next two-and-a-half years, Lonergan was the strategist and Lovett the executioner as The White Hand Gang grew its bootleg operations and fought a bloody war against the Italian Black Hand faction.

Lovett's reign as the head of The White Hand Gang ended on November 1, 1923. He was shot several times before being hit over the head with a meat cleaver by a Sicilian hit man, Will 'Two Knife' Altieri.

Peg Leg now took the helm of The White Hand Gang, determined to avenge his friend and drive the Italian Mafia from the waterfront.

A brutal three years followed, with massive profits flowing into the gang's coffers and the body count constantly mounting.

The Italian Mafia looked on nervously and decided Peg Leg had to die. They turned to an old enemy of The White Hand Gang, Al Capone.

Frankie Yale, head of The Black Hand Gang, went to Chicago and put a proposal to Capone. In December 1925, Al Capone took his son Albert to see a New York specialist to treat his mastoid infection.

On Christmas night, while his son recuperated after the operation, Capone decided to take a trip to one of his old haunts, the Adonis social club, a South Brooklyn speakeasy owned by the Italian Mafia.

That same night Richard Lonergan and his gang also decided to pay it a visit. Lonergan led a contingent of his men into the club — a deliberate visit to cause a fight with Mafia soldiers.

Around 10pm, Peg Leg Lonergan and five of his men entered the bar. According to witnesses they were in high spirits and being rude and aggressive to other patrons. In contrast Al Capone and his associates sat quietly at the back of the bar.

A fight broke out between Lonergan and three Italian men who had Irish girls on their arms. Seeing two Irish girls dancing with Italian gangsters, Lonergan kicked them out of the place, ordering the girls to "get back with the white men".

Suddenly, the lights were extinguished and gunfire was heard. In the melee, panicked customers ran for the exit. Glasses shattered, tables flew and chairs were overturned.

When the lights came on, a scene of carnage was unveiled. The police quickly arrived and found one of Lonergan's men lying dead in the street.

The trail of blood led into the club and police officers found Lonergan and his associate Cornelius 'Needles' Ferry, a native of Gweedore in Donegal, on the dance floor, shot through the head in typical Mafia execution style.

A fourth member of The White Hand Gang, James Hart, managed to escape, having been found a few blocks away crawling on the sidewalk after being shot in the thigh and leg. He was taken to the Cumberland Street hospital where he eventually recovered but refused to cooperate with police. He denied being at the club, claiming he had been shot by a stray bullet from a passing car.

The two other members, Joseph 'Ragtime Joe' Howard and Patrick 'Happy' Maloney, were apparently unaccounted for, leaving no witnesses willing to testify. Seven men were arrested in connection to the shooting, including the visiting Al Capone, but all were released on bail and the case was eventually dismissed.

The killings are generally attributed to Capone, in partnership with Black Hand boss, Frankie Yale. However, the police could not substantiate reports that Capone had personally killed Lonergan and had to drop any prosecution of him.

Capone himself insisted he had nothing to do with the killings, declaring, "I never met an Irishman I didn't like." However, on his return to Chicago, Capone continued his extermination campaign against the Irish O'Banion North Side Gang.

Al Capone was there. And it is true that he was arrested and questioned for the triple murder, since he was in town for his son's surgery. The fiercest Italian criminal of all time, who was once banished from Brooklyn by the Irish-American White Hand Gang, had now exacted his revenge and essentially put the gang into the history books.

The New York Mafiosi were grateful for Capone's assistance in Brooklyn. Many believe that if Capone hadn't triggered the violence, Lonergan and his cohorts might have walked out safely.

As it was, the White Handers had been stripped of their last important leader. The Mafia now began to exert greater control over the Brooklyn waterfront.

With the death of Peg Leg Lonergan, The White Hand Gang began to disappear from the Brooklyn waterfront, allowing Frankie Yale and eventually the Mafia Five Families to take full control.

Dwyer was never drawn to the flamboyant lifestyle of other bootleggers and as his business grew he instead reinvested his profits into warehouses, trucks and experienced men to guard his operation

11

Bill Dwyer
The King Of
The Rum Runners

BILL DWYER took to organised crime late in his life at the age of 37, but he became famous as the King of the Rum Runners. He believed the prohibition of alcohol in the United States of America was a business opportunity and he saw its unlimited earning potential.

Through treating crime as a business, he took the New York Irish mob from violence and anarchy and moulded them into a multi-million dollar operation. This made him, for a time, one of the richest men in America, if not the world.

Willian Vincent Dwyer, known as Bill, was born to Irish immigrant parents in New York's Hell's Kitchen on February 23, 1883. His parents were determined that he would not fall into the hands of the two gangs prominent at the time in the area, the Hudson Dusters and the Gophers. He, unlike many of his friends, finished public school and began working life without a criminal record.

He started his adult life as a cinema usher and then became a longshoreman on the Chelsea piers, which would open his eyes to business opportunities in the future. He met and married a local girl, Agnes Frances Cassidy, and they soon started a family. They would eventually go on to have five daughters.

It was to provide for his growing family that Dwyer used his education and natural intelligence to start his own bookmaking operation, which would prove to be highly lucrative.

In 1919 the Volstead Act was enacted bringing in the prohibition of the sale and consumption of alcohol in the United States. Dwyer sensed a business opportunity.

George J Shevlin, a childhood friend from his days in Hell's Kitchen, was the owner of a string of working men's bars around the New York waterfront. He was now struggling to stay in business, even with a flow of illegally made bootleg beer. The substandard and in some cases dangerous quality of the beer was driving away even the hardest of drinkers. In some cases. it was even killing them.

However, Dwyer thought of a solution. The American government stored vast quantities of confiscated alcohol in the many warehouses that surrounded Chelsea pier. Once Prohibition began, there were some small-scale attempts to steal this alcohol, but they were clumsy and largely unsuccessful.

Dwyer knew that a more subtle solution was needed and not just violence. Bill firmly believed that violence was unnecessary and bad for business.

Bill and Shevlin became partners. They gathered together a small group of longshoremen, all Irish and natives of Hell's Kitchen, and created a criminal gang. What set Dwyer apart from his peers was that he and Shevlin largely pursued a policy of non-violence in their attempts to obtain the liquor stored by the authorities.

They began bribing key employees and forging false permits to withdraw huge quantities of industrial alcohol which they then sold on to other bootleggers.

Dwyer was never drawn to the flamboyant lifestyle of other bootleggers and, as his business grew, he instead reinvested his profits into warehouses, trucks and experienced men to guard his operation.

As his success grew, so did the violence, eventually forcing his business partner Shevlin to leave New York. Before he did, he left Dwyer $2,500 to use in an emergency.

It was not long before he needed those funds.

Dwyer was a hands-on bootlegger who often drove his own trucks. This was to prove foolhardy and soon after Shevlin left the city, Dwyer was pulled over by two detectives not on his own payroll.

They demanded immediate payment and Dwyer used the money Shevlin gave him. Word spread among the police force and soon Dwyer was inundated with offers of assistance in return for bribes.

Dwyer created a bribery network that infiltrated the New York Police Department, the federal prohibition department, the New York political establishment and the US Coast Guard.

Dwyer soon found himself at the head of a multi-million dollar operation which he treated like a business. A business he knew he could not run on his own.

Bill's problem was he was now the largest distributor of illegal alcohol in the United States and while he controlled the New York area, once one of his trucks left to distribute bootleg booze to other parts of the country he was subject to numerous hijack attempts. He needed protection and allies.

Dwyer decided he would engage with both the Italian and Jewish mafia and seek to forge a partnership.

A good idea, but Bill had another problem, he considered himself a businessman and not a gangster. He needed a partner who had the connections and who could speak the language of the underworld.

Fate would supply a solution.

In 1924 two shipments belonging to Dwyer were hijacked. Bill used policemen on his payroll to identify the culprit. He was a man he was well acquainted with, fellow Irishman, Owney Madden.

Madden was the leader of the Hells Kitchens gang the Gophers, and just out of prison after a stretch for the murder of fellow Irish gangster, Patsy Doyle.

Madden was an immigrant of Irish descent and was nicknamed Owney 'The Killer' Madden and for good reasons.

Once he knew who was responsible for the hijacking, Dwyer sent out a message to the underworld:

"Get me Owney Madden. I want to talk to him. I've got a business proposition for him."

Madden met Dwyer at his lawyer's office in Times Square and an alliance was established to build America's largest bootlegging operation.

Madden would supply the muscle and underworld connections. In essence Madden would provide the violence that Dwyer so despised, but knew was now essential if his criminal empire was to survive.

Dwyer also sat down with the Italian Mafia boss Frank Costello and representatives of the Jewish mob. Soon a nationwide network was established, which was to be known as the 'Combine'.

By 1927 the Dwyer-Madden Combine wielded unprecedented influence in New York City. With Dwyer's business acumen, ward boss Jimmy Hines' political influence and Madden's muscle, the Irish Mob was the most powerful of all the criminal organisations in New York.

An interesting aspect of the Irish mob's organisational structure was that you didn't have to be Irish to be a member. Unlike the restrictive Italian Mafia, the Irish mob was open to anyone who was useful to them. This meant Jews, Italians and African-Americans worked hand-in-hand with the Irish Combine bosses.

The ranks of the Combine were swelled with up-and-coming gangsters from various backgrounds like Francisco Castiglia, Arthur Flegenheimer, Frank Costello, Dutch Schultz and Salvatore Lucania, better known to history as Charles 'Lucky' Luciano, who would help to extend its power throughout New York and all across America.

Feeling secure, Bill set to work using millions to create the Phoenix Cereal Beverage company. This was located on 26th Street and 10th Avenue right in the heart of his old neighborhood of Hell's Kitchen. Madden was the front man, brewing what was to become known as 'Madden's No 1 Beer'.

Madden encouraged Dwyer to bring in another partner, fellow Irishman and former taxi firm owner, Larry Fay. He would become the front man to distribute Madden's Number 1 Beer and the rum, whiskey and vodka the Combine was bringing into New York.

Madden and Dwyer also partnered with former bootlegger Sherman Billingsley at the very fashionable Stork Club on East 53rd Street.

The two Irish gangsters spread their business operations into the north part of Manhattan when they bought the Club De Luxe from former heavyweight boxing champion, Jack Johnson. They inserted their associate, Big Frenchy De Mange, as their operating partner, and changed the name to the Cotton Club, which would become one of the most famous venues in New York City.

At the Cotton Club, De Mange instituted a 'Whites Only' admittance policy, despite the fact the waiters, dancers, and headline entertainers, like Cab Calloway, Duke Ellington, Louis Armstrong, Lena Horne, Bill 'Bojangles' Robinson, and the Nicholas Brothers, were all black.

The Cotton Club was wildly successful and became a cash-cow for Dwyer and Madden, whilst allowing them to clean the massive profits they were making from their illegal activities.

Bill did not rest on his laurels and was always looking for ways to improve his bootlegging business. He travelled to Canada, England and the Caribbean to develop links with anyone who could supply him with liquor, which he could then smuggle into the US.

Bootleggers known as Rum Runners had been smuggling bootleg booze into America almost from the first day of Prohibition. This success forced public outcry and needed a response from the authorities.

This came in 1924 from both the coast guard and the federal government with increased investment to stop the inflow of illegal alcohol.

The US authorities sanctioned the construction of new, faster Coast Guard ships specially equipped to halt the alcohol trade.

Undeterred, Dwyer had the resources to adapt to this evolving landscape. Using his Longshoreman connections and the wealth he now had at his disposal, he purchased a fleet of ships that would rendezvous with the supply ships miles out at sea. The booze would then be safely transferred to Dwyer's ships.

Once his vessels reached US waters and in reach of the US coast guard, the booze was transferred to a fleet of high-powered speed boats which then delivered the illegal cargo at night.

In a bid to evade the Coast Guard, Dwyer turned to another old friend who helped him purchase hundreds of airplane engines left over from World War 1. Dwyer arranged for them to be outfitted onto his existing speedboats, to create a fleet of ships now faster than any of those available to the authorities in America. The Coast Guard might see them, but they couldn't catch them.

Just in case they did catch them, Dwyer arranged for his boats to also have steel plating and high-caliber machine guns fitted.

Once his booze-laden boats reached land they were unloaded at docks which were protected by the Local 791 of the International Longshoreman's Union, which was controlled by Dwyer and Madden.

From the docks, the liquor was moved to several warehouses, again owned by Dwyer in the New York area. When the time was right, trucks filled with illegal alcohol, and protected by convoys of Teamster members, transported the booze all over the country.

His network supplied Florida, St. Louis, Kansas City, Cincinnati, and as far away as New Orleans. Dwyer was able to smuggle large amounts of booze into New York City because he knew one simple fact: you had to bribe the police and the Coast Guard if you wanted to be successful in the bootlegging business. And that Dwyer did, handing over thousands of dollars to anyone who would accept his generosity and who was willing to turn a blind eye in return.

Paying off New York City cops was easy. The cops who didn't have their hands out for bribe money were rare. However, Dwyer was especially skillful in recruiting Coast Guard members to look the other way, when his speedboats were entering New York waters.

This success of this fleet helped Bill to acquire the lifelong nickname of 'King of the Rum Runners'.

Soon the Combine was making hundreds of millions of dollars and even the well-bribed authorities were forced to act.

In 1925, Dwyer was arrested for attempting to bribe Coast Guard members during a sting operation headed by the Prohibition Bureau.

Being convicted and imprisoned was a great shock to Bill Dwyer. He had always looked upon himself as a businessman and never considered himself a gangster.

While he was in prison, a despondent Dwyer said to one of his cell mates.

"I wish I had never seen a case of whiskey. I spent years in daily fear of my life, always expecting to be arrested, always dealing with crooks and double-crossers, and now look at me. My wife is heartbroken and I am worse than broke."

While in prison, Frank Costello and the Italian Mafia eased Madden (who was already under suspicion for the murder of Mad Dog Coll) aside and took over Dwyer's operation.

After 13 months, Dwyer was released for good behaviour. He recognised the landscape had changed and the Italian Mafia was now on the ascendancy. He was a realist and slowly began to withdraw from bootlegging, instead investing his money into legitimate businesses including sports teams, owning a football and two ice hockey teams.

Bill first purchased the Hamilton Tigers of the National Ice Hockey league and moved them to Madison Square Garden, renaming the franchise 'The New York Americans'.

With his vast wealth from bootlegging and being accustomed to paying for success, Bill's strategy for sporting success was simple — pay massive wages to attract the best players and bribe officials to win at all costs.

For example in 1927 the average hockey player was earning around $1,500 a year. Bill gave one star player, a certain Billy Burch, a three-year contract worth $25,000 a year.

Dwyer also paid off line judges to award goals if the puck touched the goal line instead of passing over the line, which was the rule.

His involvement in fixing games was legendary, a fallout from his days of bribing state and federal officials.

A story is told that at a game in 1927 in Madison Square Garden, the goal judge, whom Dwyer had on his payroll, for some unknown reason started taunting Ottawa goalie, Alex Connell. Connell responded by butt-ending his hockey stick into the goal judge's nose. Dwyer became incensed at the Ottawa goalie and Connell was told to leave town quickly after the game.

A police car took Connell to the train station and protected him until the train was safely out of town. After the train left the station, a man asked Connell if he was the Ottawa goalie, Alex Connell. Connell, afraid for his life, told the stranger no. And, as a result, he lived to play another day.

Bypassing a league rule that a person can't own two hockey teams, in 1929, Dwyer, using ex-lightweight boxing champ Benny Leonard as his front man, purchased the NHL's Pittsburgh Pirates.

In 1930 he bought the Dayton Triangles National Football League side and moved the team to Ebbets Field in Brooklyn and renamed them the Brooklyn Dodgers.

After three years of vastly overpaying his players, Dwyer began hemorrhaging so much money that he was forced to sell the Brooklyn Dodgers to two former New York Giants players, Chris Cagle and John Simms, for $25,000.

Even though he sold the team for 10 times more than he had paid for them, Dwyer estimated he still lost $30,000 in the three years he owned the team.

In 1934 Bill bought the famed Tropical Park Horse Racing Track in Miami, Florida.

The authorities — sick of Bill's record of sporting bribery — came after him and in 1935, Dwyer was indicted on a gambling charge. But Bill was able to beat the case by using expensive and clever lawyers.

However, the authorities wanted to see the end of Bill's reign of interference in the American sporting world.

Gin Joint: New York's The Cotton Club was a favourite of many gangsters throughout the 1920s and 1930s

Baby-faced Assassins: Members of The White Hand Gang, a group of Irish-American gangs in New York (see Chapter 2)

Hooch Haul: A police officer with alcohol during Prohibition

The Rum Runners: See Chapter 11 on Bill Dwyer

Lord of the Ring: John Morrissey — Boxer, Gang Boss and US Congressman (see Chapter 6)

Screen Star: Emmet Dalton — The Hollywood Outlaw (see Chapter 7)

Big Bad Jim: Jim O'Leary — The Gangster Whose Family Rose From The Ashes (see Chapter 8)

'Peg Leg': Richard Lonergan — The Man Even Al Capone Feared (see Chapter 10)

Death of a 'Mad Dog': Crowds gather near the phone booth by the London Chemists drug store at 314 West 23rd Street at Eighth Avenue in New York after the murder of Vincent Coll (inset, opposite page). Coll's funeral (below) was a lonely affair (see Chapter 9)

Dash of Rum: Bill Dwyer — The King Of The Rum Runners (see Chapter 11)

Dead in Bed: Owney 'The Killer' Madden — The Gangster Who Died Quietly In His Bed (see Chapter 12)

Smiling Jack: Jack 'Legs' Diamond — The Gentleman Gangster (see Chapter 13)

Rock and Ruler: John Patrick Looney — The Rock Island Godfather (see Chapter 15)

Saying it with Flowers: Charles Dean O'Banion — Florist To The Mob (see Chapter 14)

Shock Ending: John 'Cockeye' Dunn — The Man Who Went To The Chair (see Chapter 16)

Machine Gun Kid: George Kelly — The Tommy Gun-wielding Gangster, is arrested (see Chapter 17)

Who Shot Jimmy? Frank 'The Irishman' Sheeran — Claimed He Shot Jimmy Hoffa (see Chapter 18)

Gentle Giant: Mickey Spillane — The Last Of The Gentleman Gangsters (see Chapter 19)

Hooray Henry: Henry Hill — The Irish Goodfella (see Chapter 20)

Jimmy The Gent: James Burke — The Dapper Assassin (see Chapter 21)

Most Wanted: Whitey Bulger (above and right) — The FBI's $2m Man (see Chapter 22)

Mob Jobs: American mobster Dutch Schultz (left), who ordered the murder of 'Mad Dog' Coll; right: Italian-American mobster Johnny Torrio

They decided to revert to a tactic that had worked with another figure in the criminal world, Al Capone, and they filed a case of tax evasion against Bill Dwyer.

This time the expensive legal advice was to no avail and the sporting career of the King of the Rum Runners was soon to be over.

The charges were upheld and Dwyer was stripped of all his assets except his family home in Belle Harbor, Queens and the hockey team, the New York Americans.

With no other assets, Dwyer could no longer afford the running costs of the New York Americans. This led the National Hockey League to take temporary control of the club.

Ever the fighter, Dwyer borrowed $20,000 from Red Dutton, the manager of the team. With this he hoped to show the National Hockey League he was solvent and regain control of his club.

However, instead of paying his team's salaries, a desperate Dwyer decided to try to multiply his money in a 'craps' game. He lost the lot.

Unable to pay his team, and with no other way to raise any more capital, the NHL expelled Dwyer permanently, and took final control of the New York Americans. Broke and despondent, Dwyer retired to his Belle Harbor home.

On December 10, 1943, Big Bill Dwyer, the King of the Rum Runners, died at the age of 63. Dwyer was reportedly penniless at the time of his death, his only asset being the roof over his head.

So ended the life of a man who viewed himself as

a businessman and not a gangster, who passionately believed organised crime could be more effective if it was truly organised as a business.

A template that more violent and ruthless men would follow in the future.

12

Owney 'The Killer' Madden
The Gangster Who Died Quietly In His Bed

OWEN VINCENT MADDEN, who would later be known as Owney 'The Killer' Madden, was either the deadly enemy or close friend of anyone who was anyone in the 1920s and 30s New York criminal underworld.

Despite his nickname, he would not meet an untimely death, which was the usual fate of his many friends and enemies, but instead die in wealthy retirement at the age of 74 in his own bed. This is his tale.

Owen Madden was born on the December 18, 1891 in Somerset Street, Leeds. He was the second child of Irish immigrants, Francis and Mary Madden. He had an older brother Martin and would later have a younger sister Mary.

His father Francis Madden was an abusive drunk and habitual criminal who, in between prison spells, worked in the textile mills of Wigan and Liverpool.

It was during one of these prison spells in 1901 that Mary Madden decided to escape her abusive husband

and emigrate to America, taking her infant daughter to live with her widowed sister in Manhattan.

Mary reluctantly left her two boys, Martin and Owen, in a children's home in Leeds for a year, while she worked to pay their passage to America.

On June 4, 1902, Madden, together with his brother Martin sailed from Liverpool as steerage passengers on board the SS Teutonic. He re-joined his mother and sister in New York's Hell's Kitchen, yet another immigrant in the city's long established Irish community.

Francis Madden would never see his family again and died in March 1932.

Owen Madden was never one for a school book and aged just 12 he joined the Irish criminal gang that ruled Hell's Kitchen, The Gophers.

He later claimed to have carried out his first major crime at the age of 14 when he robbed $500 from a man he had badly beaten.

Madden rapidly rose through the ranks of The Gophers and was a fierce fighter. He was renowned for his skill with a lead pipe and guns during tussles with rival gangs.

By the age of 18 Madden had killed five men and he soon rose to become leader of The Gophers gang. A graphic description of Madden comes from Craig Thompson and Allen Raymond in their classic, *Gang Rule in New York*:

> "*Owney was not a big boy, nor a big man either, and he did not go in for much activity with his fists. He preferred an 'equalizer', or pistol, a weapon that would make all men his own size. In common with his mates, he wore the turtle-necked*

sweater and cap which was the standard raiment for a tough guy... He talked out of the corner of his mouth in the 'dese, dose and dem' dialect, a habit he never got over. The thing that marked Owney for leadership in the mobs was his utter contempt for life, his own or anyone else's."

Owen quickly gained his lifelong nickname of 'the killer' when he murdered a rival Italian gang member to celebrate becoming the leader of the Gophers. Such was Madden's bravado that as his victim lay dying he shouted to bystanders:

"I'm Owney Madden, 10th Avenue."

Given the vicious and violent reputation of the Gophers, it was no surprise no witnesses ever came forward, so Madden was never charged with the crime.

The Gophers' main income came from protection rackets, where local businesses avoided fire bombs by paying protection money. This was highly lucrative and funded an opulent lifestyle for the Gophers members.

In Madden's Gopher gang, Eddie Egan, Bill Tammany, and Chick Hyland became his chief henchman. None, however, would distinguish themselves. Tammany was soon sent away for 15 years in Sing Sing prison a maximum security correctional facility in Ossining, New York State. Hyland soon followed with a four-year term, and Egan simply dropped out of sight.

Madden, still single, was intensely jealous of any man who showed attention to his numerous girlfriends. In 1911 he shot and killed William Henshaw, a shop clerk, whose only crime was he had asked out one of Owen's girlfriends. Madden confronted him, shot him in a fit of jealous rage and left him for dead in the street.

Before Henshaw died, he told the police who had shot him and Madden was arrested, but all charges had to be dropped as, yet again, no witnesses would come forward.

Later in 1911, Madden married Dorothy Rodgers and fathered a daughter Margaret, his only known child. The marriage quickly ended in divorce.

Now the undisputed leader of the Gophers, Madden began to expand his territory coming into regular conflict with a rival gang, the 'Hudson Dusters'.

Madden seemed unassailable as the leader of the Gopher gang but his over-confidence would soon be his downfall.

On November 6, 1914 the Hudson Dusters struck back, their assassins ambushing Madden inside the Arbor Dance Hall on 52nd Street near Seventh Avenue.

Madden, his bravado fuelled by drink, walked into the dancehall alone and proceeded to strut like a peacock into the middle of the dance hall. A drunken Madden stood waiting for the music to stop. As he was a well-known criminal figure, men and women apprehensively left the dancefloor and sensing trouble made for the exits.

Witnesses claim Madden shouted:

"I won't bump anybody off tonight. I don't want to spoil youse guys' party."

Laughing at the commotion he had caused, Madden left the dancefloor and sat by the balcony drinking whiskey and people watching.

He soon attracted female admirers and as he sat entertaining them, he was confronted by 11 members of the rival Hudson Dusters gang, who had only one thing in mind — to kill Owney Madden.

Perhaps it was the drink or the notorious Madden arrogance that drove him, but Owney did not run. Instead he rose to his feet and taunted his would-be assassins:

"Come on youse guys!" he hollered. "Youse wouldn't shoot nobody! Who did youse ever bump off?"

Madden and the Dusters drew their weapons and in the ongoing gunfight, Owney was hit six times.

Miraculously Madden survived and when he was questioned later by the police as he recovered in hospital, he refused to tell the authorities who shot him. When asked he replied:

"It's nobody's business but mine who put the slugs in me. The Boys will get them."

Sure enough within days, three of his would-be assassins from the Duster Gang were dead.

While Madden recuperated from his wounds, the leader of the Dusters, William Moore, better known as 'Little Patsy Doyle' made his move to usurp the Gophers and establish himself as the criminal overlord of Hell's Kitchen.

He spread a rumour that Madden's wounds would mean his criminal career was over and that he would soon leave New York.

Doyle's hatred of Madden was not confined to a desire to end his power; there was a more human element to it. He was intensely jealous of the fact that Madden had stolen his girlfriend, Freda Horner.

When Madden left hospital it was clear that he had no intention of leaving New York or giving up control of Hell's Kitchen.

A war now raged between the Gophers and Doyle's Hudson Dusters.

As the body count rose, Madden met with members of the Dusters and provided evidence that Doyle was in fact a police informant. This ensured he lost all support from his gang and a peace was brokered on the condition that Doyle was to be eliminated.

Madden planned his murder in partnership with Gopher lieutenants, Johnny McArdle and Art Biedler.

Women were Doyle's downfall and Madden used this to his advantage. On November 28, 1914 Madden's ex-girlfriend Margaret Everdeane and Doyle's estranged fiancée Freda Horner met at the Ottner Brothers' bar at 41st Street and Eighth Avenue.

Madden arranged for Everdeane to telephone Doyle and she told him that Freda wanted to reconcile with him. A besotted Doyle believed them and arranged to meet Freda at the bar and arrived at around 8.30pm.

When he entered the bar, he asked for Freda and was told she was in the bathroom. As he waited, Maddens henchmen McArdle and Biedler approached him and opened fire. Doyle, mortally wounded, staggered out of the bar and died on the steps outside.

The investigating police arrested both Margaret Everdeane and Freda Horner as material witnesses.

The police, determined to break the Gopher gang, pressured both Everdeane and Horner, who cracked under interrogation and they both implicated Madden in the murder; his luck had run out.

The authorities moved quickly and arrested Madden. This was the 57th time he had been arrested and apart from one traffic violation he had always walked away a free man, but the police were determined to get a conviction this time.

The Gophers put pressure on Everdeane and Horner and they eventually recanted their testimony, but the judge was having none of it and he maintained their earlier accusations were valid. Because of this Madden was found guilty and sentenced to 20 years in Sing Sing prison. His associates were also found guilty; McArdle received 30 years, and Biedler 18.

Owney Madden was released on bail after nine years and quickly saw the landscape had changed dramatically.

His old gang the Gophers no longer existed, its members were either dead, in jail or had joined other crime gangs such as the White Hand gang, growing as a result of Prohibition.

Looking for a foot on the new crime ladder, he joined the Dutch Schultz organisation as a lowly soldier. However, because of his close friendship with ex-Gophers Larry Fay, Vincent 'Mad Dog' Coll and Legs Diamond he quickly rose through the ranks of the Shultz mob and in 1931 he left to set up his own gang.

Madden employed a young man as his personal driver, a certain George Raft who would go on to be a major film star, famous for his uncanny portrayal of gangland figures.

A girlfriend of Madden at this time was the film star Mae West, whom Madden would help financially throughout her life.

West would describe Madden in her memoirs as:

"Sweet, but oh so vicious."

Madden's criminal model was simple — he and his

gang would hijack trucks ferrying bootleg booze from New York, to the thirsty mid-west and then sell on the contents. While this was highly lucrative, it was also dangerous.

After hijacking liquor shipments belonging to Big Bill Dwyer, a war seemed likely. However, Dwyer, a very intelligent criminal, decided to talk rather than pull the trigger and suggested that Madden become his partner and become his muscle to stop any further hijacks.

Madden quickly introduced Dwyer to his friend George 'Big Frenchy' DeMange and suggested they funnel the enormous bootlegging profits into legitimate businesses such as nightclubs.

They would go on to purchase and run the Cotton Club where patrons poured into Harlem from all over New York to listen to performers such as Duke Ellington, Louis Armstrong and Lena Horne.

The Cotton Club had originally been owned by the black prize-fighter Jack Johnson and was a mecca for New York nightlife in the 1930s. Madden and DeMange forced Johnson to sell up.

While the club continued to showcase the best in black entertainment, a 'whites only' patron policy was introduced. All non-whites, be they employees or entertainers, were forbidden to enter by the front door and no black patrons were allowed.

Madden also gave the owners of the Stork Club an offer they could not refuse and began to hold court at the most exclusive nightclub in New York.

The Stork Club was the base for the gossip columnist, Walter Winchell, and was a popular venue for New York society's elite.

Madden himself soon became a media personality and an iconic face of Prohibition-era crime and corruption.

His wealth and reputation soon put him at loggerheads with the rising Italian crime syndicates headed by Lucky Luciano and Frank Costello.

When his business partner Bill Dwyer was imprisoned in 1931, Madden knew Costello would soon make his move to take over Dwyer's operations.

Ever the realist, Madden got out of bootlegging alive and used a payoff from Costello to enter the world of boxing becoming a promoter. Again working with DeMange the pair managed some of the most famous boxers of the era, Rocky Marciano, Max Baer and Primo Carnera.

In February 1932, under pressure from Lucky Luciano, Madden was involved in the murder of his close friend and ex-Gopher, Vincent 'Mad Dog' Coll, who had a $50k bounty on his head.

Madden set up his old friend, promising a peace summit and Vincent was assassinated by two of Luciano's men at a drug store on 8th Avenue.

Madden was now distancing himself from the New York crime scene and concentrating on his boxing promotions business. He took a particular interest in Primo Carnera.

Carnera was a giant of a man but not a particularly good boxer and an unlikely world title contender.

Madden ensured, through fight-rigging, that Primo Carnera earned an undeserved shot at the world heavyweight title.

In 1933 he fought the then-champion Jack Sharkey, knocking him out in six rounds. The fight was so clearly rigged that calls for an inquiry soon became thunderous.

The wily Madden thought of a solution — he dropped Carnera and arranged for another of his fighters, the famous German heavyweight Max Baer, to challenge him. Baer did not need a fight fixed and won easily in their bout on June 14, 1934.

Madden was now under severe pressure from the Mafia five families. Their control of the police led to Madden being imprisoned briefly for a parole violation. Owney decided it was time to leave New York.

Looking for a new life he had begun visiting Hot Springs, Arkansas, which under the corrupt mayor, Leo P McLaughlin, had become a safe haven for bootlegging, prostitution and gambling.

Madden was now in his 40s and suffering chronic ill health due to his numerous gunshot wounds; he needed a rest.

Despite its criminal links, Hot Springs was also known for its health-reviving waters and was just the place for Madden to recuperate.

Madden left for the destination in 1934 and soon began romancing a local gift shop clerk, Agnes Demby. They would marry on November 26, 1935 and remain married for the rest of Owney's life. Agnes was no fool and knew all about his past and future plans.

It has been speculated that ill health was not the only reason that led Madden to move to Hot Springs. It was unusual for a mobster to give up his operations peacefully. Given his relationship with Frank Costello and Lucky Luciano, it is possible they may have brokered a peace deal and exit package.

Lucky Luciano also had close links with Hot Springs' Mayor McLaughlin, and Municipal Judge, Vern Ledgerwood.

Could Luciano have encouraged Madden to move to Hot Springs to take advantage of their corrupt nature? It is certainly plausible, as Madden eventually helped both McLaughlin and Ledgerwood run their own criminal syndicate.

While both denied any involvement by Madden, it was common knowledge that Owney had supplied them with the wire service they used to bring racing results from all over the country to the Hot Springs bookmakers.

In 1940, feeling rejuvenated, Madden officially resurfaced and opened a hotel, spa and casino and kept his hand in the local underworld, but managed to stay out of trouble and the headlines.

Madden also owned a controlling interest in the Southern Club, a luxurious and lucrative hotel and gambling establishment on Hot Springs Central Avenue. Hardly lying low.

His growing empire included interests in numerous other gambling and prostitution establishments.

Madden kept out of the papers but the Southern Club became the recreational hideaway of the who's who of organised crime. Frank Costello, Meyer Lansky and Lucky Luciano all visited Madden regularly and in the open, enjoying holidays with their families.

The Southern Club was also used for organised crime summits and as a venue for dispute resolution.

Perhaps rest and recuperation wasn't the reason Madden moved to Hot Springs after all.

The English-born Madden finally became an American citizen in 1943 but would not give up his British passport until 1950.

In post-war America, the authorities began to look more closely at organised crime. The corrupt Hot Springs McLaughlin political machine was voted out of power in 1946. However, through bribery and police corruption Madden's rackets still flourished and the mob elite continued to 'holiday' in Hot Springs.

Throughout the 50s and early 60s, Madden was a familiar figure in Hot Springs, becoming patron of numerous charities and easily recognisable in his trademark Irish cloth cap and scarf. No police action was taken against him but the tide was turning.

With the election of John F Kennedy as President and the appointment of his brother Robert as Attorney General, state action on organised crime cranked up.

Late in 1961 a federal investigation concluded that Hot Springs Arkansas was "the site of the largest illegal gambling operation in the United States".

Despite his denials of involvement, Owney Madden was summoned to appear before the US Senate committee on organised crime under Arkansas senator, John McClellan.

In a session of robust questioning, true to his Gopher roots, Owney Madden told the authorities nothing of consequence or substance, frequently pleading the Fifth Amendment.

The exasperated authorities could not pin anything on Madden and he avoided any charges.

Three years later in 1964, the authorities took its first major steps in shutting down illegal operations in Hot Springs, closing numerous gambling joints and brothels.

This was of little consequence to Owney Madden, who died on April 24, 1965 following a bout of emphysema. He died in his own home, one of the few major gangsters of his time to end his life quietly in bed, unlike his many friends and enemies. He was survived by his loyal wife Agnes. They had no children.

A peaceful end for Owney 'The Killer' Madden who ended up entertaining the mob on their holidays.

Once it was apparent who was behind the spate of liquor heists, all protection was removed from the Diamond brothers and it was open season for revenge and retribution

13

Jack 'Legs' Diamond
The Gentleman Gangster

J ACK 'LEGS' DIAMOND became an iconic figure of
the Prohibition era, his notoriety and private life
showcased both the glamour and brutality of the bootlegger gangsters.

There are numerous theories on why he was called
'Legs' Diamond. One is that it was because he was a flamboyant member of the New York underworld, owner of
the Hotsy Totsy nightclub and a keen dancer.

However, the most likely reason is because of his ability to outpace his rivals who tried and failed to kill him
numerous times.

Diamond survived a number of attempts on his life
between 1916 and 1931, causing him to also be known as
the 'clay pigeon' of the underworld.

Diamond himself put his survival down to the fact
that he believed:

"The bullet hasn't been made that can kill me".

As we will see, this was not true.

Jack 'Legs' Diamond was born Jack Moran on July 10,
1897 to Irish immigrant parents in Philadelphia, Pennsylvania.

His parents Sara and John had left Kilrush, Co Clare in 1891, settling in Philadelphia.

Jack was their first child, followed in 1899 by a brother, Eddie. The Moran children struggled academically and had little parental care, as John worked to raise his family and his wife Sara became bed-ridden as a result of severe arthritis.

Jack was to lose his mother when he was 16 when Sara died from complications of a bacterial infection.

Following the death of his wife, John Moran decided to move his family to New York in the Irish-American enclave of Brooklyn.

Left to their own devices the Moran brothers drifted out of school and joined a Jewish and Irish-American street gang called The Boiler Gang. Jack then changed his surname to Diamond.

Jack's first encounter with the authorities was just two months after his mother's death when he was arrested for robbing a jewellery store in February 1914. This was to be the first of 12 arrests over his life of crime.

Found guilty he was detained in a juvenile reformatory. He was released in 1917, as America entered World War 1 and was immediately drafted into the army.

His war record was far from noble; he served less than a year before going AWOL. He was quickly arrested and sentenced to three to five years in the Army prison, Fort Levenworth, for desertion.

On his release in 1921, Diamond and his brother moved to Manhattan to work for Charles 'Lucky' Luciano, then an up-and-coming gangster. Diamond did a variety of odd jobs for Luciano, who introduced him to his mentor, Arnold 'The Brain' Rothstein, a gambler and financial wizard.

Rothstein was the man who arranged for the Chicago White Sox players to throw the 1919 Baseball World Series and was the most powerful gangster in the city at the time.

Jack was so trusted by Rothstein that he became his bodyguard and as a reward he was given a cut of his very successful heroin operation.

Jack married Alice Kenny, who, while disapproving of his lifestyle, stuck by him until his death.

The Diamond brothers became rich but greedy and decided to branch out into the booming and highly profitable bootlegging business. Looking for an instant return rather than set up their own business, they decided to cut in on established players.

Their plan was to hijack deliveries of illegal alcohol owned by the Irish gangsters 'Big Bill' Dwyer and Owen Madden the friend of Vincent 'Mad Dog' Coll.

They would then sell this on to rival gangs, a dangerous idea as Madden was business partners with Dutch Shultz, 'Lucky' Luciano and Myer Lansky, a triumvirate who controlled the Prohibition racket in New York.

Once it was apparent who was behind the spate of liquor heists, all protection was removed from the Diamond brothers and it was open season for revenge and retribution.

On October 24, 1924, as Diamond drove his blue Dodge Sedan uptown along Fifth Avenue, he pulled up to the intersection at 110th Street (the boundary of both Harlem and Dutch Shultz's territory).

A large black Limo pulled alongside Diamond. According to eye witnesses, a shotgun appeared from the back window of the limo and opened fire.

Hit by the gunfire, Diamond was able to drive himself to nearby Mount Sinai Hospital where doctors removed pellets from his head, face and feet.

It was then that he acquired another nickname, The Clay Pigeon. This was because he was so hated by other mobsters, he always had a target on his back.

Diamond now knew that to survive he would need the protection of a major player.

He and his brother turned to Jacob 'Little Augie' Orgen (Orgenstein), a Jewish gangster who ran several rackets in Lower Manhattan and was one of the few people who was not now a sworn enemy of Jack's.

Jack became Orgen's bodyguard and in turn, Orgen cut him in on his bootlegging and narcotics rackets. The relationship went well until October 15, 1925, when an attempt was made to kill both Orgen and Jack Diamond.

Orgen was fatally shot in the head, and Diamond was shot twice on the right side. He was taken to Bellevue Hospital, where emergency surgery was performed and he eventually recovered.

The police interviewed Diamond, but again he refused to identify any suspects or help the investigation in any way, leading police to suspect Diamond was an accomplice. They charged him with murder but, without proof, the charge was soon dropped.

The murder was never solved, but it's commonly believed the assassins were hired by or included notorious mobsters Louis 'Lepke' Buchalter and his partner Jacob 'Gurrah' Shapiro, who were seeking to move in on Orgen's rackets.

It's unknown if Diamond was part of the plot, but after his release from the hospital, Diamond was given Orgen's bootlegging and narcotics operations by Buchalter and Shapiro while they gradually took over Orgen's other rackets.

Jack was now immensely wealthy and he became a regular on the nightclub circuit. His picture was constantly in the papers with his mistress Marion 'Kiki' Roberts, the famed nightclub singer and dancer.

His wife Alice, whom Diamond married in 1920, did not seem to mind. Her apartment was filled with Diamond's pictures. One over the fireplace had the words 'My Hero' underneath it. She told the press Kiki had her man's attentions, but she had him legally.

Diamond and Roberts became a celebrity couple. He was not portrayed as a gangster, but as a wealthy man-about-town with the glamorous Roberts on his arm.

He soon became part-owner of the Hotsy Totsy Club on Broadway. The club had a back room where Diamond frequently settled business disputes, usually by shooting his adversaries to death, then carrying them out as if they were drunk — but the good times were not to last.

Diamond's luck began to change when on July 13, 1929, three drunken dockworkers started a brawl in the Hotsy Totsy Club bar.

They began to attack the bar manager and Diamond and one of his henchmen, Charles Entratta, decided to end the fight and protect their employee from harm.

Soon shots rang out and the three dockworkers lay dead. Before the police arrived Diamond and Entratta decided that with so many witnesses it was best if they made themselves scarce and they went into hiding.

Diamond knew that if any of the witnesses were to testify he would end up in jail so he decided to do what he did best and arranged to kill them all.

Over the next few weeks, the club bar tender, cashier, hat check girl and one waiter simply vanished off the face of the earth. The police knew Diamond was guilty, but could not prove it.

With everyone out of the way, Diamond and Entratta felt safe as they thought that nobody now could possibly harm them so they calmly turned themselves into the police.

Diamond was never charged, but the constant police pressure was on and he soon closed the club and moved to Greene County in upstate New York.

In his absence, Dutch Shultz and Owney Madden moved quickly to absorb his rackets. Diamond was told if he ever returned to New York he would be killed.

Following a failed visit to Europe to obtain new sources of alcohol, he returned to New York and took a suite of rooms at the Hotel Monticello on Manhattan's west side and began trying to re-establish his rackets in the city.

But 'The Clay Pigeon' again had a target on his back and on October 12, 1930, Diamond was attacked and wounded by three men who forced their way into his hotel room and shot him five times.

Diamond was taken to the Polyclinic Hospital in Manhattan, where he recovered yet again and was discharged on December 30.

On April 21, 1931, Diamond was arrested for hijacking, but was released on bail. A week later, Diamond was shot and wounded once more, this time at the Aratoga Inn in New York, a notorious hangout for gangsters. When Dutch Shultz heard he had survived, he was reported to have said:

"Can't anybody shoot this guy so he won't bounce back up?"

While still in the hospital, New York State Troopers seized more than $5,000 worth of illegal beer and alcohol from Diamond's hiding places in Cairo and at the Aratoga Inn. He was arrested and charged.

In August, Diamond went on trial for bootlegging. He was convicted and sentenced to four years in state prison. Diamond appealed his conviction and was released on bail as he awaited the outcome of that appeal.

On December 17, he was unexpectedly acquitted and that night he and his family and a few friends celebrated in the Rainbow Room of the Kenmore Hotel, Albany's best hotel.

At about 1am on December 18, Diamond left the party and went to visit his mistress, Marion 'Kiki' Roberts. According to reports, shortly after his arrival at Roberts' home, a large black car which had been parked down the street much of the evening, pulled up in front of the house. Two men got out and entered the main door using a key. They quickly went upstairs and entered the bedroom.

Diamond was asleep on the bed in his underwear. While one man held down Diamond, the other shot him three times in the head.

His luck had run out. The Clay Pigeon had finally been killed. Diamond was buried in Mt. Olivet Cemetery in Queens on December 23, 1931.

There was no church service or graveside ceremony. No underworld figures came or sent flowers.

So who ordered the killing of Jack 'Legs' Diamond?

Despite speculation linking people such as the gangster Oley Brothers or corrupt officers in the Albany Police department, the most likely candidate has to be Diamond's old enemy, Dutch Schultz. He had tried to kill Jack so many times it seems he finally got lucky.

On July 1, 1933, Alice Kenny Diamond, was found shot to death in her Brooklyn apartment. It was speculated that she was shot by Diamond's enemies to keep her quiet, but that was never confirmed. Like Diamond's murder, Alice's was never solved.

As for Marion Roberts, she went back to showbusiness in Boston where she would perform under the billing as 'Jack (Legs) Diamond's Lovely Light o' Love'.

14

Charles Dean O'Banion
Florist To The Mob

IKEBANA, the Japanese art of flower arranging (also known as kado — "the way of flowers"), began with monks in Buddhist temples and then was taken up by members of the aristocracy and the Samurai warrior class.

It is said that Japanese Samurai practiced *ikebana* to reach a state of peaceful concentration and mindfulness before going into battle. Charles Dean O'Banion, one of the Prohibition era's most notorious gang leaders, employed a similar technique, when he purchased a flower shop as a front for his criminal activities and became known as the 'Florist to the Mob'.

O'Banion was born on July 8, 1892 to Irish-American parents in the small town of Maroa in central Illinois.

Dean, as he was to become known, grew up in a loving family, a block west of Route 51 in the north end of the town. He was a childish prankster in school who continually teased his classmates.

In 1900 tragedy struck when Dean's mother was diagnosed with tuberculosis. She would die a year later and the nine-year-old O'Banion was devastated. He had loved his mother very much, writing her letters daily and bringing her flowers while she was in hospital.

His father was equally devastated and decided to start a new life with two of his children Dean and his brother Floyd in Chicago. Two older children, Frank and Ruth, remained with their aunt.

They settled in the heavily Irish neighbourhood of Kilgubbin (now called Goose Island) in Chicago's north side. The area was also known as 'Little Hell' and notorious for its high crime rate.

A devout Catholic, O'Banion was an altar boy and sang in the Cathedral choir. However, Dean took to crime from an early age.

The boys of Kilgubbin used to play bumper riding, which was trying to get a free ride on a trolley car. One day Dean was trying this when he fell and a trolley car ran over his foot. He would be left with a limp for the rest of his life and gain a new nickname, 'Gimpy', but given his notorious temper, this was seldom said to his face.

Dean had a real zest for life and while a limp would have held back many children, he was made of sterner stuff and his enthusiasm, energy and charm more than made up for his disability.

In his teens, he formed a street gang with three others from the neighbourhood with whom he would continue to associate with throughout his life: Earl 'Hymie' Weiss, Vincent 'The Schemer' Drucci and George 'Bugs' Moran.

The Chicago of the period was, according to Mayor 'Big Bill' Thompson, a "wide open city". Wide open for rackets such as prostitution and gambling, and wide open for violent competition among gangsters. Bombings and murder would be met with token official resistance but more often than not they would be settled by uneasy truces among the rival gangs.

At 16 Dean took a job as a barman at a local bar, McGovern's. He served beer while singing, a distraction that allowed his friends to pick the pockets of the drunk and distracted patrons.

O'Banion also drugged patrons' drinks, known as "slipping a Mickey Finn". When the drunk and drugged patrons left the club, O'Banion and his pals would pounce and rob them.

In 1909, Dean got caught stealing stamps and a bottle of perfume from a drugstore. He ended up spending six months inside the Bridewell Boys Reformatory for burglary.

In 1911, he received a three-month sentence for carrying a concealed weapon.

These would be the only times he would be imprisoned in his criminal career which was about to take off.

O'Banion, along with his friends Earl 'Hymie' Weiss and George 'Bugs' Moran, joined The Market Street Gang, which specialised in theft and robbery for the city's thriving black market. The boys later became 'sluggers' — thugs hired by a newspaper to beat newsstand owners who did not sell their paper.

The Market Street gang started out working for the *Chicago Tribune*, but later switched to the rival *Herald Examiner* because of a more attractive offer from newspaper boss, Moses Annenberg.

Through Annenberg, the gang allegedly met safecracker Charles 'The Ox' Reiser, who taught them his trade. The gang also met the political bosses of the 42nd and 43rd wards through Annenberg, and they were later hired to use violence to help steer the outcome of elections.

The newspaper wars were a good warm-up for O'Banion's work as a bootlegger when Prohibition came into effect in 1920, O'Banion was one of the first to recognise the potential it offered organised crime. He quickly established relationships with beer suppliers in Canada, and also struck deals with whiskey and gin distributors.

Chicago, with its large population of immigrants from Ireland, Germany, Italy and Eastern Europe, was a town that loved its beer, wine and liquor. Almost from the start, O'Banion's North Side gang was at odds with the Italian-led South Side operation to feed this demand.

The first recorded liquor hijacking in Chicago was carried out by O'Banion and his gang on December 19, 1921.

O'Banion quickly formulated the structure of his North Side Gang, eliminating all competition and took control of the city's North Side and the Gold Coast, a wealthy area of Chicago on the northern lakefront. At the height of his power, O'Banion was supposedly making about $1 million a year profit on booze alone.

During another incident, O'Banion and his men stole more than $100,000 worth of Canadian whiskey from the railroad yards, while in yet another event, O'Banion broke into the Sibly Distillery and stole 1,750 barrels of bonded whiskey.

For brains, he relied on his second-in-command, the clever and ruthless Hymie Weiss, who was said to have been the only man Capone feared (though Wild Bill Lovett and Joey Aiello must have also kept him up at night.) What made him an especially dangerous adversary was that because Weiss knew he was dying of cancer, he had little or nothing to lose.

The North Side Gang wasn't exclusively Irish. None of O'Banion's ultimate successors were of Irish descent, but its ethos and culture was.

They were less disciplined than other gangs. Even as O'Banion's men were raking in millions from Prohibition, they continued mugging, safecracking and committing robberies. Freelancing was also a frequent occurrence and rarely discouraged.

In 1920, 'Papa Johnny' Torrio, the head of the predominantly Italian South Side mob (later known as the Outfit), and his second-in-command, Al Capone, met with all the city's bootleggers to work out a system of territories. Torrio wanted to run bootlegging as a business and avoid any violent turf wars. He also believed that if everyone worked together, they could maximise their political power.

The usual method of operation for the Italian Syndicate was for all members to pay Torrio a portion of the profits as a tribute for political influence and protection from other criminals.

Johnny Torrio wanted to keep the Irish gangster inside their group and he even offered to make an exception in the case of the North Side gang and not require any tribute. O'Banion agreed to join and to consolidate their new partnership, the two sides exchanged shares in each other's businesses. Torrio got shares in some of O'Banion's breweries and in return, O'Banion was bought in to some of Torrio's distilleries and gambling dens.

The other gangs accepted the agreement, and O'Banion was ceded control of the North Side, including the desirable Gold Coast. The North Siders now became part of a huge Chicago bootlegging combine. As part of this agreement, O'Banion supplied Torrio with some of his thugs to help them win the mayoral election of Cicero, a suburb of Chicago that served as Torrio's base.

In 1921, O'Banion married Viola Kaniff and bought an interest in William Schofield's River North Flower Shop, near the corner of West Chicago Avenue and North State Street.

He needed a legitimate front for his gangland activities and it soon began to serve as the headquarters for the North Side gang.

There was an additional benefit to owning the shop as it allowed O'Banion to indulge his lifelong love of flowers.

He became known as an excellent flower arranger, and Schofield's quickly became the florist of choice for mob funerals, which was a thriving business!

The shop was directly across the street from Holy Name Cathedral, and he and Weiss attended Mass almost daily.

O'Banion lived with Torrio's deal for about three years before becoming dissatisfied with it.

Since the rigged election, Cicero had become a gold mine for the South Siders and O'Banion wanted his piece of the action.

To avoid a war, Torrio granted O'Banion some of Cicero's beer rights and a quarter-interest in a casino called 'The Ship'.

O'Banion, ever the entrepreneur, then convinced a

number of speakeasies in other Chicago territories to relocate to the area he controlled in Cicero.

This move had the potential to start a war and Torrio attempted to convince O'Banion to abandon his plan in exchange for some South Side brothel proceeds. O'Banion refused because, as an Irish Catholic, he objected to prostitution.

War was not far off. The Genna Brothers, who controlled 'Little Italy' in Chicago's downtown, began selling their whiskey in the North Side, O'Banion's territory.

O'Banion complained about the Gennas to Torrio, but Torrio did nothing. In retaliation, O'Banion started hijacking Genna liquor shipments. He also raised the tension between himself and the Gennas by insisting that Angelo Genna pay in full a $30,000 debt he owed to 'The Ship'.

This was a step too far for the brothers and the Gennas decided to kill O'Banion.

However, as the Genna crime family was Sicilian, it owed loyalty to the *Unione Siciliane*, a mutual benefit society for Sicilian immigrants and a front organisation for the Mafia.

They appealed to Mike Merlo, president of the Chicago branch of the *Unione*, for permission to kill O'Banion.

However, Merlo disliked violence that impacted negatively on business and refused to allow the hit. The Gennas could do nothing but watch as O'Banion continued to chip away at their territory.

In February 1924, O'Banion made a move against his South Side rivals by unsuccessfully trying to frame Torrio and Capone for the murder of North Side gang member, John Duffy.

This plan would fail and he had now made enemies not only of the Gennas but the South Side gang and a certain Al Capone.

The last straw for Torrio, however, was O'Banion's treachery in the Sieben Brewery raid, a brewery in which both O'Banion and Torrio held large stakes.

In May 1924, O'Banion learned the police were planning to raid the brewery on a particular night.

Before the raid, O'Banion approached Torrio and told him he wanted to sell his share in the brewery, claiming the Genna brothers had intimidated him and he wanted to leave the bootleg business.

Torrio agreed to buy O'Banion's share for half-a-million dollars. On May 19, as O'Banion already knew, the police swept into the brewery. O'Banion, Torrio and numerous South Side gangsters were arrested. O'Banion got off easily because, unlike Torrio, he had no previous Prohibition-related arrests and he had also bribed the police. Torrio, however, had to bail out himself and six associates and faced serious charges.

Knowing he had been double-crossed, Torrio demanded O'Banion return the money he had given him but O'Banion refused.

Torrio had lost the brewery and the $500,000 in cash (more than $6 million in today's money) he had given O'Banion. Johnny Torrio could overlook many things to keep the peace and profits flowing, but public humiliation was unforgivable. He now had enough of the North Siders and backed the Genna brothers' pleas for war against O'Banion. Permission was sought for a hit.

The Chicago Godfather Mike Merlo again refused to

sanction the death of O'Banion, but Merlo had terminal cancer and died on November 8, 1924. With Merlo gone, the Gennas and Torrio were free to kill O'Banion.

Using the Merlo funeral as a cover, a Mafia hitman, Frankie Yale from New York City and other gangsters visited O'Banion's flower shop to discuss floral arrangements. However, the real purpose was to kill O'Banion.

On the morning of November 10, 1924, at about 11:30, O'Banion was clipping chrysanthemums in Schofield's back room when Yale entered the shop. With him were Torrio gunmen John Scalise and Albert Anselmi.

"Are you from Mike Merlo's?" O'Banion asked, holding out his right hand to Yale.

As he greeted Yale with a handshake, the two men with Yale stepped forward and fired two bullets into O'Banion's chest, two in his face, and two in his throat. Yale released his grip and O'Banion fell back against a display case door and then onto the floor. He died instantly.

Though O'Banion had served as an altar boy and given generously to the Church, the Archbishop decreed that he could not be buried in consecrated ground.

Nevertheless, thousands of mourners defied the cold of a late day in January and turned up for his funeral, lining the streets and falling into step with the cortege. O'Banion's graveside ceremony was attended by all manner of politicians, and his extravagant rites set the standard for all gangland funerals to follow.

O'Banion was buried in Mount Carmel Cemetery in Hillside, Illinois, under the direction of Sbarbaro & Co. Undertakers, 708 N. Wells, Chicago, directly four blocks west of O'Banion's flower shop.

Dating back to 1885, this Italian firm handled many of

the funerals for reputed gangsters, including the lavish funeral for Mafia Godfather, Mike Merlo.

At the crowded cemetery, Father Patrick Malloy of St. Thomas of Canterbury church recited prayers for the kind person he knew in O'Banion. Father Malloy stated that: "One good turn deserves another", a reference to O'Banion helping needy and poor families on the Northside and the refusal of the Archbishop to allow O'Banion consecrated ground.

Months after O'Banion was laid to rest, his family was eventually allowed to rebury him on consecrated ground elsewhere in the cemetery.

The O'Banion killing sparked a brutal five-year gang war between the North Side gang, now headed by George 'Bugs' Moran, and the South Side mafia.

Torrio would escape an assassination attempt in 1925 and turn over his operation to Al Capone.

O'Banion's friend and ally Hymie Weiss, who was fingered as one of those who tried to kill Torrio, was gunned down in 1926.

In 1929, in an effort to put the North Side gang, led then by Bugs Moran, down for good, seven of the North Side mobsters were killed in the infamous St. Valentine's Day Massacre, but Moran would survive through to the end of Prohibition in 1933.

15

John Paul Looney
The Rock Island Godfather

THE line between fact and fiction is often broken when discussing the lives of famous gangsters. It really is an example of 'when the fiction is more interesting than the facts, print the fiction', and one such case is the film, *Road to Perdition*.

I can give the film some leeway as it never claims to be an autobiography, but the main villain John Rooney, played by the screen legend Paul Newman, is obviously moulded on John Patrick Looney, the Rock Island godfather.

John Patrick Looney served as the model for John Looney, a major character in Max Allan Collins' graphic novel, *Road to Perdition*. The character was renamed John Rooney and portrayed by Paul Newman in Sam Mendes' 2002 film adaptation.

In the film, the actual war between Looney and his long-term loyal lieutenant Dan Drost is the basis for the conflict between Michael Sullivan (played by Tom Hanks) and Paul Newman's character.

The major flaw with the film is that it is set in 1931, six years after Looney was incarcerated for murder.

Nonetheless, it is an excellent film and does explore some of the traits of a complex and intelligent man who moved from being a young lawyer and family man to a ruthless millionaire criminal godfather, a man who at one time rivalled the power of Chicago mobsters, Johnny Torrio and Al Capone.

John Patrick Looney was born in Ottawa, Illinois on October 5,1865, the first child born to newly arrived Irish immigrants. Little is known of his childhood, which does not appear to have been deprived or unduly traumatic. He moved to Rock Island, Illinois when he was 19 to work on the growing railroad as a train dispatcher. He soon grew bored and left to become a superintendent for the telegraph office.

An intelligent and hardworking young man, he studied at night for a law degree and was admitted to the state bar in 1889.

He also married and soon had two daughters and a son. He seemed the picture of respectability, but behind this façade of normality, lay a deep-seated desire for wealth and power.

His legal career began with his partner, Frank H. Kelly, but this was not profitable enough for him and he soon abandoned purely legal ways of making his fortune.

His first foray into illegal activity came in 1897 when he was accused of conspiracy to defraud the city council, by using inferior materials in the allegedly fraudulent 24th Street storm drain scheme.

He was found guilty, but his conviction was overturned on appeal.

As with many ambitious young lawyers, he saw politics as an avenue for progress. He joined the Democratic

Party and in 1898 he ran for office as a Democratic candidate for the Illinois state legislature. He narrowly lost the election, blaming his defeat on the influential *Rock Island Argos*, a local newspaper which was highly critical of him during the race.

To ensure he could control his own publicity in the future, Looney, now heavily involved in the criminal world, decided to set up his own rival newspaper, the *Rock Island News*.

In 1905 Looney bought an old closed club, the Mirror Lounge. He established his law office on the first floor and refurbished the second floor to publish the *Rock Island News*.

John sent news to his younger brothers William and Jeremiah to leave Ottawa and join him in Rock Island and run the paper for him.

Looney used his new paper to attack his rival, the *Rock Island Argus* and as a weapon against his enemies. He threatened to expose the deep dark secrets of the Rock Island elite. He would demand large fees to kill salacious stories and anyone who refused was publicly shamed in the pages of the *Rock Island News*.

Looney's empire now included match fixing, prostitution, illegal gambling, and extortion.

A gambling joint and brothel was set up in the basement of his office. This ensured he had all his business interests in one place. He would also have his henchmen photograph his patrons with prostitutes and threaten to publish the photographs in the *Rock Island News*, unless a cash payment was provided.

By 1908 Looney was dangerously over-extended and his business empire was on the verge of collapse. Desperate for money he was forced to sell a controlling interest in the *Rock Island News* to a local businessman, W.W. Wilmerton.

Looney wanted the cash to shore up his criminal empire and then influence Wilmerton to print his views in the paper. However, Wilmerton was no stooge and an independent man.

He wanted a clean slate and decided to shut down the *Rock Island News* and set up a new paper, the *Tri-City Morning Journal* and move its operations to a different location.

This angered Looney and the night that Wilmerton shut down the paper, a bomb exploded, destroying the printing press.

In November of that year, two mysterious fires would also destroy the Mirror Lounge. The first fire on November 2 caused $32,000 worth of damage to the building, destroying the saloon, now run by Looney associate Dan Drost.

The second fire started the day before the insurance was cancelled, causing $75,000 worth of damage to the Mirror building.

Looney was accused of arranging the fire by Dan Drost, but in the later years he admitted to helping Looney set the fire and collect the insurance money.

With Looney unable to publish his newspaper for a year after he sold it, he was left powerless in Rock Island politics, since he was unable to blackmail its residents. He did, however, continue his criminal activities.

Looney resumed his publishing from the garage on the side of his house called the 'The Roost' in 1909. Looney moved his newspaper again that year to the upper storey of his mansion overlooking the Mississippi river.

Looney used the relaunched *Rock Island News* on February 8, 1909, to personally attack Wilmerton and his family on the front page.

Wilmerton took these personal attacks in his stride but finally cracked when Looney ran an edition which said he had details he would soon publish which would see Wilmerton go to jail.

The running feud would lead to a bizarre showdown and a gun-fight involving both men.

On the morning of February 22, 1909, they had a loud argument on the streets of Rock Island. Looney claimed that, as the men parted, Wilmerton shot him in the back.

Both men were arrested and during the investigation there were grave doubts about Looney's wound. Police Chief L. V. Eckhart called a local doctor, Dr. B. J. Lachner, but Looney wouldn't let Lachner examine him.

Looney called in his personal physician, Dr. G. G. Craig, Sr., then refused to let Chief Eckhart be present during his examination.

When the chief wanted to examine his clothes for bullet holes, Looney declined.

Dr. Craig's statement was ambiguous:

"I cannot tell from the nature of the wounds whether Looney was shot in the back or not." He saw two penetrations in his back but was unsure what to think. *"The bullet, I believe, did not penetrate any vital organ. It passed out about three inches from the point it entered,"* said the doctor.

"I do not regard the wound as serious."

Wilmerton claimed that Looney fired first and through the bluster of counter-accusations and no concrete evidence, neither man was ever charged.

Looney continued to grow the new incarnation of the *Rock Island News* and his criminal empire, controlling all the gambling and prostitution in the area.

In March 1921, one of Looney's key lieutenants, Anthony Billburg, was arrested for extortion.

Looney approached the Mayor of Rock Island Harry M Schriver, who was not adverse to mob dealings and asked him not to prosecute Billburg. Perhaps the bribe was not sufficient because he refused.

An enraged Looney immediately published an article on his front page with the headline

"Schriver's Shame! Spent Night and Day in Peoria in Filthy Debauch with Ethel: Deeds that Would Shame a Dog!"

The Mayor immediately had every newsboy who sold the paper arrested and thrown in jail. He also issued a warrant for Looney's arrest.

The police found Looney and delivered him to the mayor's office, where Schriver beat Looney so severely he required an extended stay at St. Anthony's hospital.

Looney's henchmen arranged for a political rally for a certain Harry McCaskrin, who was running for election as State Attorney. McCaskrin was also a lawyer and regular contributor to the *Rock Island News*.

As Looney lay in hospital, McCaskrin began a fiery speech attacking Mayor Schriver and enraging the crowd. Two nights of rioting in downtown Rock Island followed, with passions heated by Looney henchmen. Two innocent bystanders were slain, eight people shot and dozens others wounded. The sheriff, panicked by the extent of the riot, phoned Illinois Governor Charles Deneen asking for state intervention.

The riots prompted the Governor to declare Martial Law in Rock Island and ordered the National Guard to the city.

Throughout the night there were minor disturbances, which were only resolved whenever the National Guard troops made an appearance.

After the riots, raids were carried out on prostitution houses. All public gatherings were banned, and all saloons were closed. The *Rock Island News* was also shut down by Mayor Schriver.

After Looney recovered from his beating he decided that it was too dangerous for him and his family to remain in Rock Island and he elected to move to a luxurious ranch he had purchased in New Mexico. He would remain in comfortable exile until 1917.

While Looney had been away, crime did not stop and in his absence others formed their own gangs, many headed up by his former loyalists.

They had sampled the delicious taste of power and sharing it with Looney, if he returned, was not an appealing prospect.

His key lieutenants, however, reluctantly stayed loyal for the time being but wanted a greater share of the profits.

On his return, Looney's empire, now co-managed by his son Connor, continued to grow and expanded dramatically with the onset of Prohibition. He had control of approximately 150 gambling dens and brothels. Looney also extorted protection from local business in collaboration with corrupt police officers and politicians including his old rival Mayor Schriver, whose corruption easily outshone his earlier hatred of Looney.

Despite being at the zenith of his power, the seeds of his doom were being sown all around him.

First a local saloon keeper Bill Gabel stood up to Looney's extortion rackets. Gabel had been paying protection money to Looney for years, but refused to pay an increase.

Gabel and Looney eventually worked out a compromise deal, but Gabel prepared to set Looney up. Gabel started paying by cheque rather than the usual method of cash. Gabel decided to hand over evidence of these cheques to the Federal authorities, thinking this would bring down Looney. He met FBI agents in the Como Hotel on the night of July 31, 1922.

However, corrupt local police tipped off Looney and he decided Gabel had to die. Retribution was virtually instantaneous, as Gabel was gunned down in his bar just hours after meeting the FBI agents, murdered by the bullets of Looney's henchmen.

The *Rock Island Argus*, a long-time enemy of Looney, now began running front page stories exposing Looney's criminal empire and demanding he be brought to justice. The *Argus* lambasted the community for having allowed gangsters to gain control of Rock Island. In return, Looney's paper published bizarre and outlandish articles implicating the *Argus* in Gabel's murder.

The final act that really brought down Looney was war with his own trusted lieutenants — Anthony Billburg, George Holsapple, Dan Drost and George Buckley. They had been loyal for years but now decided that it was time for a change and that Looney had to go.

On October 6, 1922, they ambushed Looney and his son Connor outside the Sherman Hotel in downtown

Rock Island. When John Looney got out of the car and saw Billburg's black Maxwell parked across the street, he shouted at his son to run, while he ducked behind his car.

Young Connor Looney, who was by now a seasoned criminal but with an unpredictable and violent reputation, drew his gun and turned to face Billburg's men. He died in a hail of bullets. His distraught father fled the scene unhurt.

Two weeks later the authorities acted, all stills, speak-easies, and brothels under Looney's control were closed down, and his house was raided for weapons. Mayor Schriver and the former police chief were arrested and later convicted on a charge of vice protection conspiracy.

John Paul Looney was indicted for the murder of William Gabel and for running a theft ring which spanned several states, but again tipped off by corrupt officials he first fled to his home town of Ottawa, Illinois and then to his ranch in New Mexico.

He was apprehended there in November 1924. He was convicted in 1925 of "conspiracy to protect gambling, prostitution and illicit liquor traffic in Rock Island".

Looney was later charged and convicted of the murder of William Gabel. There was no direct evidence to link Looney to Gabel's murder, only the testimony of Looney's henchmen who traded testifying against him in exchange for leniency.

John Paul Looney, once the undisputed godfather of Rock Island, was sentenced to 14 years in Statesville prison in Joliet. He served eight-and-a-half years.

Looney was nearly 70 years old when he was released from prison on humanitarian grounds. He did not return to Rock Island but instead he moved to Texas and died in 1947 of tuberculosis in an El Paso sanatorium. A sad end for a man who strived for and held so much power.

16

John 'Cockeye' Dunn
The Man Who
Went To The Chair

VERY few of the men you have read about here died peacefully in their beds. Most ended their lives violently at the hands of rivals or as the victims of retribution for their own mis-deeds. However, the man I would like to talk about now, John 'Cockeye' Dunn, didn't die at the hands of his fellow mobsters, but executed by the authorities, electrocuted in Sing Sing prison, guilty of a gangland murder.

John Dunn was born on August 24, 1904, to Irish immigrant parents, Tom and Kitty Dunn. They had left the west coast of Ireland in search of a better life and settled in the New York borough of Queens.

Tragedy was to strike the family when Tom Dunn, a merchant sea man, was lost on a voyage in 1915.

As a teenager Dunn was quickly nicknamed Cockeye due to a lazy eye. Like many of his contemporaries in 1920s Queens, Dunn turned to crime as a route out of grinding poverty and he joined local gangs.

Still a teenager, he was arrested for petty theft and assault but his first custodial sentence was yet to come.

At the age of 19 Dunn was arrested for robbing an illegal card game and sentenced to two years in the infamous Sing Sing prison, a maximum security correctional facility in Ossining, New York State.

On his release, Dunn vowed to be cleverer in his criminal career and rather than staying a petty thief he instead became an enforcer for mid-ranking Mob boss, Eddie McGrath.

McGrath not only controlled Hell's Kitchen but was the organiser of the muscle behind the International Longshoremen Association's (ILA) control of the New York waterfront.

Founded in 1892 the ILA began as a legitimate labour trade union in the great lakes area and spread to New York in 1914. The aim of the union was originally to ensure fair treatment for dockworkers from their employers.

The New York ILA was quickly taken over by the Mob. While both the Italian and Irish gangs wanted dominance, the ILA eventually became the stronghold of the Irish faction, manipulated by vicious mobsters such as Joseph P Ryan, who would become its President.

The mob control of the ILA was simple but effective. Dockworkers were not hired by qualifications or skills, the only requirement was that you agreed to pay a tribute to the hiring boss called a 'Stevedore'.

Twice every day each man who wanted to be hired would line up on the New York loading docks and await selection. Then the 'Stevedore' would choose those lucky enough to get a job. Every man had to agree to pay a percentage of his wage to the 'Stevedore', who as a member of the ILA, would then pass this onto the 'Head Stevedore'.

They would then pay the Mob boss, who in the 40s waterfront happened to be Dunn's boss, Eddie McGrath.

McGrath was the ILA president Joseph P Ryan's main man and now Dunn was part of the organisation, which was highly lucrative for them all. Dunn would develop even closer relations with McGrath when he married his sister.

Dunn was now mixing in illustrious criminal circles and became friends with powerful Mob bosses such as Joe Adonis and Meyer Lansky, who was known as the accountant to the Mob and the man who along with Lucky Luciano helped create the corporate structure of organised crime in America.

In 1937 Dunn and McGrath were arrested for the murder of a trucker who had offended the ILA. Mob lawyers and political connections ensured that the charges were dropped due to a lack of evidence.

Dunn now decided to form a union of his own and in 1938 with the help of Joseph P Ryan and Meyer Lansky, he created the labour union Local 21510, Motor and Bus Terminal Checkers, Platform and Office Workers. This 'union' oversaw Mob-based racketeering on Manhattan's Lower West Side throughout the early 40s.

Meyer Lansky was keen for Dunn to help him use dock workers to import heroin and cocaine into the United States. Dunn was at the height of his power and enjoying the life his criminal activity was funding when his aggressive nature ruined it all.

A 'stevedore' by the name of Andrew Hintz was skimming the take from the dockworkers at Pier 51 and rather than have another union enforcer handle it, Dunn decided to deal with Hintz himself.

At 7.40am on January 8, 1947, Andy Hintz was shot six times on the steps outside his apartment as he left for work.

As Mob hits go, this was pretty unsuccessful as Hintz survived the attack and was taken unconscious to St Vincent's Hospital.

Before he lost consciousness Hintz had told his wife he recognised the men who tried to murder him and said one of them was John Dunn, an old colleague who he had worked with on the New York waterfront.

The authorities arrested Dunn immediately. Over the next three weeks Hintz drifted in and out of consciousness and during a moment of clarity on January 11, Hintz gave a dying declaration in which he identified John Dunn, former prizefighter turned Mob hitman Danny Gentile and Mob henchman Andrew Squint Sheridan as the men who had shot him.

A dying declaration is a statement under American law made by a person who is conscious and knows that death is imminent, about the circumstances of his death that can be introduced into evidence during a trial.

Two days later, Hintz, near death now, gave another dying declaration, because in his first it was felt he did not express clearly enough his belief that he was about to die. Unluckily for Hint this time he was clearly dying and the authorities acted upon his declaration.

First on January 24 the police arrested Andrew Sheridan in Hollywood, Florida. Then at the end of March, Danny Gentile decided to turn himself in. He turned up at the Assistant District Attorney's office with his lawyer in tow. Now all three suspects were in custody and held without bail being offered.

The state's main witness was Hintz's widow Maisie, who was now under police protection, as it was feared Eddie McGrath and the Irish mob would intervene to ensure Dunn's acquittal.

The trial began on December 4 before Judge George L Donnellan, whose claim to fame was having sent film star Mae West to the woman's workhouse for ten days on a charge of acting in what was judged an immoral play on Broadway.

The jury was soon selected and despite the efforts of the best lawyers the Mob could afford, on December 31, 1947, the jury found all three men guilty of murder. Judge Donnellan sentenced them to death in the electric chair.

In an effort to save their lives, both Dunn and Gentile offered to become informers and provide evidence against the ILA and their waterfront rackets in exchange for commuting their death sentences to life imprisonment.

The deal for Dunn fell through. His information was considered false by the authorities and the only evidence they believed concerned individuals now dead and beyond their reach.

Dunn and Sheridan were now condemned to die in the electric chair.

They both spent their final days in the building in Sing Sing prison known as Death House. This was in fact a prison within a prison. The building was self-contained with its own hospital, kitchen, visitor's room and exercise yard.

Death House had 24 single cells and three additional cells for women facing the death penalty.

Dunn and Sheridan spent their last night in an area called the 'Dance Hall', reserved for your last hours. A corridor known as the 'last mile' connected the Dance Hall with the execution chamber.

On the morning of July 7, John 'Cockeye' Dunn walked down the Dance Hall into the execution room escorted by seven wardens and the prison Chaplin. There he came face to face with the warden of Sing Sing, the state electrician, two doctors and 12 witnesses appointed by the state.

John Dunn was strapped into the electric chair and the state electrician attached the electrodes to his shaven head.

The warden stepped forward and read out the sentence of death. He then asked John Dunn if he had any last words. He did not and a final prayer was said.

At 11pm on July the 7th 1949 the Warden signalled for the execution to begin and so ended the life of John 'Cockeye' Dunn. The witnesses left after the two doctors confirmed his death.

Andrew Sheridan was executed just after John Dunn. However, Danny Gentile had been reprieved the day before. The Governor of New York, Thomas E Dewey, commuted his death sentence to life imprisonment.

This was as a result of a letter from the District Attorney Frank Hogan, in which he claimed that Gentile had co-operated with the state and provided useful information that had helped fight criminal activity on the New York waterfront.

As a result of the Gentile evidence, Dunn's brother-in-law and close associate, Eddie McGrath, had to flee the New York area. His mentor Meyer Lansky set him up as an ILA organiser in Miami and ensured the authorities did not pursue him for his crimes in New York. He would spend the rest of his life in the Florida sun.

John Dunn was raised in poverty and used his criminal activities to rise in society. But as we have seen that society reaped a terrible vengeance upon him.

While based in Memphis, George and his gang were soon distributing illegal booze all across the south, through Tennessee, Mississippi, Texas, Oklahoma and New Mexico

17

George 'Machine Gun' Kelly
The Tommy Gun-wielding Gangster

ONE of the most evocative nicknames of the Prohibition-era gangsters has to be George 'Machine Gun' Kelly, a man who defied all the usual stereotypes of Irish-American gangsters.

He was not born into poverty or from a broken home or raised in the Irish-American heartlands of the east coast.

Instead, George Kelly Barnes was born into a loving middle class Irish-American family in Memphis, Tennessee. He also stood out from the pack of fellow gangsters by creating his own PR and image.

For a man with such an infamous nickname of 'Machine Gun', George never killed another human being — not easy for a bootlegger, kidnapper and serial bank robber.

George Kelly Barnes was born on July 18, 1895 to Irish immigrant parents who had moved from Chicago in the early 1890s and established a comfortable life in Memphis. Little is known of his childhood, but at age 17 he enrolled to study agriculture at Mississippi State University.

Kelly did not enjoy a happy time at university. Constantly in trouble with the faculty, he did not enjoy the course and his grades suffered. The highest grade he achieved was a C+, which was for good physical hygiene.

Not surprisingly, he did not last long at university and soon dropped out. He began work as a cab driver and it was during this time he met his first wife, Geneva Ramsey.

Aged just 19, George married Geneva and they soon had two boys. He worked long hours as a cab driver in Memphis to try and feed and clothe his young family, but he soon found this difficult. Struggling financially, he gave up his job and went to work for a local bootlegger and began a life of petty crime. While George enjoyed the rewards of crime and his newfound notoriety, his wife was less impressed and they separated and eventually divorced. When Geneva was interviewed in later years, she would go on to tell the *New York Times*, she divorced him because he was:

"Running in bad company."

During the 1920s Kelly was an established bootlegger, first working for others, but soon creating his own operation. While based in Memphis, George and his gang were soon distributing illegal booze all across the south, through Tennessee, Mississippi, Texas, Oklahoma and New Mexico.

As a major player in the bootlegging industry, George began to receive more and more attention from the authorities and despite large bribes he could not avoid regular raids.

As his notoriety grew, he was conscious not to bring shame on his family, who led a respectable life. He began to refer to himself as George R Kelly and would be known by this name for the rest of his life.

Tired of the police, he decided to leave Memphis and head to the west coast with a new girlfriend.

In 1928, Kelly was arrested outside Tulsa, Oklahoma charged with attempting to smuggle alcohol onto an Indian reservation. He was found guilty and on February 11, 1928, he began his three-year sentence in Leavenworth Penitentiary, Kansas.

It's reported he was a model prisoner and was released early for this good behaviour. This, however, did not mean he was going straight. George used his time in prison to cultivate relationships with notorious bank robbers such as Charlie Harmon, Frank Nash, Francis Keating and Thomas Holden.

He wanted them to give him an insight into their trade of bank robbery. He grew so close to Keating and Holden, it was rumoured he had helped them in their successful escape bid.

Upon his release, Kelly moved to Oklahoma City where he went into partnership with fellow bootlegger Steve Anderson. Kelly quickly fell for Anderson's mistress Kathryn Thorn, already a seasoned criminal in her own right.

Thorn had a long record of criminal activity stretching from armed robbery to prostitution. Twice married she had only recently lost her last husband Charlie, a well-known bootlegger, who had died in suspicious circumstances.

The official cause of death was recorded as suicide, but it was rumoured that Kathryn was to blame. She had been witnessed threatening to kill him only days before his death, but no charges were ever brought against her.

George and Kathryn were married in Minneapolis in September 1930. His new bride soon bought him a belated wedding gift of a machine gun.

Kelly, who had up until then never had any interest in firearms, was soon taking long country walks with his wife and practising with his new gun.

Some have speculated that Kathryn's purchase of the machine gun was premeditated, as she wanted George to move on from bootlegging and graduate to bank robbery.

Up until he married his wife, George was content to be a small-time crook, earning a good living but never attracting too much attention. His new wife and the machine gun would soon change all that.

From 1930 to 1933 George used his machine gun to carry out a series of bank robberies from Texas to Mississippi.

Many historians believe that Kathryn created the 'Machine Gun Kelly' image. She had a habit of taking spent gun cartridges to clubs frequented by the criminal fraternity and distributing them as souvenirs from 'Machine Gun Kelly'. She was also the mastermind behind Kelly's crime spree, which led the FBI to publish wanted posters, describing Kelly as an 'Expert Machine Gunner'.

A legend had now been born.

In 1933 George and Kathryn had now grown tired of the small sums they had been gathering from bank raids which were now becoming harder and harder to execute. They knew they needed a bigger score and decided to move into kidnapping and picked a large target indeed. They decided to kidnap noted businessman and oil tycoon, Charles Urschel.

On July 22, 1933, George, carrying his trademark Tommy gun with his accomplice Albert Bates, barged into to the Urschel mansion in Oklahoma City. They found the Urschels playing bridge with another couple. George brandished his Tommy gun shouting:

"Everyone do as I say or I will blow your heads off."

This is when their first problem began, as George didn't know which of the two men Charles Urschel was and they were not inclined to tell him.

Undeterred, George and Albert tied up the women and bundled the men outside into their getaway car. By the side of a quiet country road, they frisked them for identification and when they discovered that one of the men was Urschel's close friend, Walter Jarret, they robbed him of the $51 in his wallet and left him on the deserted road.

They then sped off, taking their kidnap victim to their hideout in rural Texas.

Three days later, a ransom note appeared via Western Union at the home of Urschel's friend, J.G. Catlett, demanding $200,000 for the release of Charles Urschel.

E.E. Kirkpatrick, a friend of the Urschel family, was enlisted to deliver the ransom, which was to be in denominations of $20 bills.

On July 30, he left the money as instructed near the LaSalle Hotel in Kansas City.

The following day Urschel was released near Norman, Oklahoma, and casually walked into a local restaurant to call for a cab.

It appeared as if everything had gone smoothly. Urschel was back with his family and George and Kathryn had the ransom money.

However, things would soon start to unravel.

After splitting the ransom money with their accomplices, George and his wife both dyed their hair to conceal their identities and began travelling around America, lavishly spending their share while trying to stay ahead of the authorities.

Kelly thought it was the perfect crime. He had been careful to ensure Urschel was blindfolded the entire time and he used a ranch owned by his mother-in-law not known to the authorities.

However, this was Kelly's first attempt at a major kidnapping and he failed to take into account that the authorities had liaised with the Urschel family and noted the serial numbers of the $20 bills used in the ransom.

This ensured that any time the serial numbers showed up in a transaction they could track any of the gang. Also George had not counted on the sharp mind and keen senses of his victim.

Urschel was an intelligent man, and despite being blindfolded throughout his ordeal, he made sure that his fingerprints were spread everywhere. He also counted his footsteps to various areas when blind-folded, and made note of the audible sounds of his surroundings. This was all useful in the FBI's investigation which was led by a young J Edgar Hoover.

Without Urschel's calm intelligence gathering, perhaps Kelly would have gotten away with the kidnapping.

Working with the FBI, Urschel noted that one hour after he was blind-folded, he could hear and smell oil fields nearby with the oil fields spaced 30 minutes apart.

From the several clues that Urschel was able to provide, the FBI deduced that the kidnapper's hideout must have been in the vicinity of Paradise, Texas.

The FBI, convinced that George 'Machine Gun' Kelly was the culprit because of the Tommy gun used in the initial kidnapping, knew that his mother-in-law had a ranch in the area.

On August 12, 1933, the FBI raided the property and arrested Kelly's mother-in-law, Shannon, her husband and son.

Kelly's accomplice Albert Bates was apprehended the next day in Denver after he swapped some of the marked bills used in the ransom at local banks.

Still, George and Kathryn evaded capture. The couple made their way to Memphis to stay with a trusted friend, John Tichenor.

On the morning of September 26, 1933, FBI agents supported by local police officers made their move, acting on a tip off.

They forced their way in and it was later reported that as they did so, a badly hungover George Kelly, still in his pyjamas, cried out:

"G-Men, please don't shoot."

His wife Kathryn was still asleep.

The couple were quickly flown to Oklahoma City to stand trial. The next day the FBI raided a ranch in Coleman, Texas. This belonged to Cassey Earl Coleman, who was arrested along with Will Casey. The FBI found $73,250 of the Urschel ransom money hidden in a cotton field on the ranch.

Both men would serve time in Leavenworth for aiding George Kelly.

On October 12, 1933, George and Kathryn Kelly were convicted and sentenced to life imprisonment.

Their trial made history for many reasons, not least because it was the first kidnapping trial after the Lindberg Law which had made kidnapping a federal crime. This also meant the involvement of J Edgar Hoover's FBI who contributed so much to Kelly's arrest.

The trial was also the first federal criminal trial in the United States in which film cameras were allowed.

Kelly was sent to Leavenworth in Kansas, and Kathryn was incarcerated in a federal prison in Cincinnati.

Kelly was arrogant towards prison officials and bragged to the press that he would escape, break out his wife and they would spend Christmas together.

It was decided that these threats should be taken seriously and in August of 1934, Kelly along with his accomplices Albert Bates and Harvey Bailey, were transferred from Leavenworth by train to Alcatraz. Arriving on September 4, 1934, they would be among the first groups of prisoners. Kelly became AZ#117.

Alcatraz saw a change in the previously belligerent Kelly. He was to spend 17 years here and earned the nickname Pop Gun Kelly. This was not because of his association with the Tommy gun, but because of his exemplary behaviour in prison.

He was noted once again as a model prisoner, spending his time working in the laundry, the prison offices and even as an altar boy.

The warden at the time, James Johnston, would later tell that Kelly never gave him any trouble during his time there. He did, however, suffer from bouts of depression when he received letters from his family.

Warden Johnston would also disclose that throughout his time in Alcatraz, Kelly wrote regularly to his kidnap victim, Charles Urschel. In these letters George explained his remorse and begged him to intercede and support his requests for parole. Urschel never replied to these letters.

Kelly was fondly remembered by his fellow inmates in Alcatraz where he would regale them with tall tales of his escapades as Machine Gun Kelly.

In 1951 Kelly was quietly transferred back to Leavenworth in Kansas where he'd first met the bank robbers that helped push him into a life of crime two decades earlier.

He died of a heart attack at Leavenworth on July 18, 1954, his 59th birthday, and is buried at Cottondale Texas Cemetery with a small headstone marked 'George B. Kelley 1954'.

His wife Kathryn was released from prison in 1958 and took a job at an Oklahoma hospital as a bookkeeper. She lived in relative anonymity in Oklahoma under the assumed name 'Lera Cleo Kelly' until her death in 1985 at the age of 81.

So ended the life of 'Machine Gun Kelly', the Tommy gun-wielding gangster who never killed anyone.

Hoffa believed that Frank Sheeran was his loyal and trusted right-hand man. It was this relationship with Hoffa that would involve Sheeran in one of America's enduring crime mysteries

18

Frank 'The Irishman' Sheeran

The Man Who Claimed He Shot Jimmy Hoffa

GANGSTERS and their crimes have fascinated Hollywood from the heyday of cinema to modern times and an acclaimed thriller is *The Irishman*, the story of Irish-American mob hitman and Teamster Union official, Frank 'The Irishman' Sheeran.

Directed by Martin Scorsese, the movie is based on Charles Brandt's 2004 book, *I Heard You Paint Houses*. This was Sheeran's confessional and documented his life in the Teamsters and as a Mafia hitman.

Frank Sheeran was born on October 25, 1920 in Darby, Pennsylvania, a working class Irish enclave on the outskirts of Philadelphia.

Frank's parents where devoutly religious and his formative years witnessed the harsh era of the Great Depression.

Seeking adventure and an escape from poverty and only 17 he lied about his age to enlist in the American Army. Given that he was now 6' 4" and weighing 290 pounds, the enlisting sergeant didn't take much convincing to sign him up.

Originally assigned to the military police, Sheeran craved more action and in 1941 was transferred to the 45th Infantry Division under General George S Patton.

The 45th was nicknamed the 'Thunderbirds' by the allies and the 'killer division' by the enemy, as they showed no remorse or gave no quarter as they swept through Europe.

During WW2, the average American infantry man served 100 days in combat. Frank Sheeran faced the enemy for a total of 411 days. He first experienced combat during the Italian campaign including service in the invasion of Sicily, the Salerno landings, the Anzio campaign and the bloody and brutal battle for Monte Cassino.

He also fought in the Allied landings of southern France, the Battle of the Bulge, the crossing of the Rhine and invasion of Germany.

Frank Sheeran enjoyed his service in World War 2 and was quoted as saying:

> *"I had fifty days lost AWOL, mostly spent drinking red wine and chasing Italian, French and German women. However, I was never AWOL when my outfit was going back to the front lines."*

He later confessed that it was during this period he developed a callousness for human life. In his book, *I Hear You Paint Houses*, he revealed a fascinating insight into his war years.

Having spent almost treble the average number of days in combat, it's perhaps charitable to assume he was fatigued and brutalised by the war. Sheeran tells of an incident when a close friend of his had just been killed by a German soldier who then decided to surrender. Sheeran was having none of this and instead, as he describes in his book, "sent him to hell too". He did this on a number of occasions and witnessed this behaviour in other GIs.

Sheeran also killed prisoners on the orders of his superiors and did not flinch, preparing him for his life in organised crime.

The war certainly brutalised many survivors and is it any wonder many remained silent on their experiences. Sheeran believed the war dehumanised him and removed any compassion he had for human life. He told his biographer of an incident in the Harz Mountains, the setting of so many Brothers Grimm fairytales and this story certainly has a dark ending.

Sheeran's unit came upon a Wehrmacht mule train carrying food and drink up the mountainside. The female cooks were first allowed to leave unmolested, then Sheeran and his fellow GIs ate what they wanted and soiled the rest with their waste.

Then the Wehrmacht mule drivers were given shovels and ordered to dig their own shallow graves. Sheeran later joked that they did so without complaint, likely hoping that he and his buddies would change their minds. But the mule drivers were shot and buried in the holes they had dug. Sheeran explained that by then:

"I had no hesitation in doing what I had to do."

The 'Thunderbirds' also participated in the 'Dachau Massacre', when American soldiers, shocked by the conditions on liberation of the concentration camp, allegedly participated in the killing of more than 35 SS guards.

When Allied soldiers liberated the camp, their reactions varied from being shocked, horrified, disturbed, and angered by the masses of dead. Their anger grew as they found the combativeness of some of the remaining German guards, who had initially fired on them and had refused to surrender.

The Dachau liberation reprisals were a series of incidents in which German prisoners of war were killed by American soldiers and concentration camp internees at the Dachau concentration camp on April 29, 1945.

In the days before the camp's liberation, SS guards at the camp had forced 7,000 inmates on a death march that resulted in the murder of many from exposure and shooting.

It is unclear how many SS members were killed in the incident but most estimates place the number killed at around 35 to 50.

The US Army began an investigation, under the Seventh Army's assistant inspector general, Lt Colonel Joseph Whitaker.

On June 8, 1945 his report concluded that a court martial should be considered for those involved.

However, General George Patton, who had recently been appointed the military governor of Bavaria, decided that all charges should be dropped and the matter was closed.

Frank was now free to go home.

A day before his 25th birthday, Private Frank Sheeran was discharged from the United States Army and re-entered civilian life. How would a man who had witnessed and been part of so much brutality adjust to civilian life?

He returned to Darby and began to work as a trucker. Seemingly settled down, he married his wife Mary and three daughters — Mary Anne, Peggy and Dolores — were born in the years that followed.

However, a life of quiet domesticity was not for Sheeran. To make extra money for his growing family he turned to crime. Due to his physical presence and military experience, Frank soon came to the attention of local Mafia boss, Russell Bufalino, becoming his sometime bodyguard and a murderer for hire.

Sheeran explained how he operated as a hitman and later confessed to over 40 hits for the Bufalino family:

"I looked like a broken down truck driver with a cap on, coming to use the bathroom. I don't look like a Mafia shooter."

This was how he carried out his most infamous murder, that of Mafia Don, Joseph 'Crazy Joe' Gallo, at Umberto's Clam House in New York's Little Italy.

Gallo's death, in front of his wife and young daughter, remained a mystery until Sheeran confessed to the killing at the end of his life.

He also told how he was assisted by IRA man John 'The Redhead' Francis, who drove the getaway car.

Frank Sheeran explained how each Mobster was given different tasks during a hit, so that noone knew the entire details. He said:

"If one person did everything, they'd be shot afterwards to keep them quiet. So everyone had a role without anyone else knowing. It meant there wouldn't be a massacre afterwards."

As Sheeran's involvement in crime increased, this caused a tension in his private life. While his family never knew or suspected of his involvement in organised crime, his absences began to take its toll on his marriage. Frank and Mary separated and were later to divorce. Frank would marry again and have another daughter, Connie.

Mafia Don Russell Bufalino was now Sheeran's mentor and he introduced him to a man who was to become his great friend, James 'Jimmy' Hoffa.

Hoffa was a working-class icon who turned the Teamster union into a nationwide movement, before falling from grace and going to jail for racketeering.

Hoffa wanted to solidify his control of the union by getting rid of his enemies in the rank and file, what he called rebels.

Hoffa believed that the only way the working men and women of his union could prosper was by solidarity. Basically everyone had to be on the same page at the one time. When other union members were trying to make deals for themselves, where they would promise labour in exchange for money, Hoffa wanted those people gotten rid of and he talked to his new friend, Russell Bufalino.

Guess who Bufalino would recommend to do this dirty work? Frank was now introduced to Hoffa.

The first words Hoffa said to Sheeran were:

"I heard you paint houses."

This was Mafia slang for a hitman as the blood goes over the walls when the victim is shot, and those words where later to become the title of Sheeran's confessional memoirs.

Sheeran replied to Hoffa that he was also a carpenter, which meant he also disposed of the bodies himself.

Hoffa and Sheeran became great friends and Frank became a Teamsters official, but in reality he was Hoffa's bodyguard and personal hitman.

Hoffa believed that Sheeran was his loyal and trusted right-hand man. It was this relationship with Hoffa that would involve Sheeran in one of America's enduring crime mysteries.

Hoffa had involved the Teamsters with organised crime from the 1950s onwards and had been facing criminal investigation since then.

With clever lawyers and amazing bravado, Hoffa avoided jail for years. That was until the election of John F Kennedy and the appointment of his younger brother, Robert F Kennedy, as Attorney General.

Robert Kennedy had been publicly frustrated by the earlier attempts to convict Hoffa while working as a legal counsel and now set out to get his man. In 1961, Robert Kennedy set up the 'Get Hoffa Squad' of prosecutors and investigators.

This was a small Justice Department unit of lawyers and investigators assembled to uncover and prosecute any unlawful activity within organised labour. By the time they disbanded, their conviction rate was impressive.

Yet Robert Kennedy's campaign against union corruption, and Hoffa in particular, raised questions about the role of an Attorney General in prosecuting crimes. The constant investigations resembled a vendetta to those who suspected Kennedy's motives. Some thought the Attorney General was dogging Hoffa out of personal spite.

Others questioned the ethics of the nation's chief law enforcement officer aggressively investigating an individual before evidence of wrongdoing presented itself. Civil libertarians were concerned by Hoffa's never proven but steady protests that he was a victim of illegal surveillance and paid government perjurers.

Hoffa was eventually convicted of attempted bribery of a grand juror in 1964 and sentenced to eight years. He spent three years fighting his conviction and when his last appeal failed in 1967, he began his sentence.

On December 23, 1971, less than five years into his 13-year sentence, Hoffa was released from prison when President Richard Nixon commuted his sentence to time served.

While Hoffa was in jail, Sheeran had continued to work for the Teamsters and the Bufalino family as both a union official and a hitman.

As a Teamster official, he saw Hoffa try to reassert his control over the union and as a member of the Bufalino operation, he also saw how the Mafia did not want this to happen.

It was alleged that in Hoffa's absence, the Teamsters' pension fund had been supporting Mafia projects such as building in Las Vegas and the Mob was now afraid Hoffa's bid to take over the union would lead to these funds drying up.

Despite his loyalty and friendship with Hoffa, Sheeran was ordered by Bufalino to kill him. Sheeran would later confess to the author of his memoirs, that despite Hoffa being a dear friend, you didn't defy orders. If he hadn't killed him, he'd have been shot himself.

In his book, Sheeran tells how on July 30, 1975, he met Hoffa in the parking lot of the Red Fox restaurant in Bloomfield township, a suburb of Detroit.

Hoffa had told his wife he was going to iron out a few issues with two Mafia leaders, Anthony Giacalone and Anthony Provenzano.

Sheeran maintains that he and Hoffa left the car park with mobster, Sal Briguglio. Witnesses confirmed later that they saw Hoffa leave the parking lot in the back of a car with two other men and a driver.

Sheeran expanded that they drove to a house in downtown Detroit. Hoffa and Sheeran got out. Briguglio left with the driver, Chuckie O'Brien.

Sheeran and Hoffa went inside and it is here that Frank carried out the hit on Jimmy Hoffa, shooting him dead.

Sheeran confessed that while he killed Hoffa, another Mafia gang disposed of the body, ensuring it was cremated so that no trace would be left behind.

Frank may have murdered his good friend Hoffa, but that didn't prevent him from wearing his watch. His daughter stated that one of his most prized possessions was a gaudy watch given to him by Jimmy during a benefit in Frank's honour.

According to his daughter Dolores, he wore the watch until the day he passed away.

Sheeran never spoke about his mobster past until his final days. Wanting absolution for his horrific crimes, the hitman chose to disclose the secrets of his past to former prosecutor and crime writer, Charles Brandt, in the last five years of his life.

One of his final acts was to appear on video tape to confirm that the finished manuscript of his confessional *I Heard You Paint Houses* was a true and faithful account of his life.

Just six weeks after reading the manuscript, Frank Sheeran passed away at the age of 83 on December 14, 2003. He had never spoken of his mobster past to his family.

I Heard You Paint Houses was published on May 24, 2005 and was made into a blockbuster movie by Netflix in late 2019.

Not only does it explore the death of Hoffa but the film also contained explosive revelations surrounding the death of John F Kennedy. In the book, Sheeran claimed to have supplied the guns to the men who assassinated the president.

After his death, his daughter Dolores and her husband Michael cleared out Sheeran's apartment and discovered another great passion of his — clothes. She explained:

> "He was always dressed like something out of Gentlemen's Quarterly. He had 200 designer suits, 100 pairs of shoes. I know now that he killed his friend Jimmy,' Dolores said. 'He had no choice, he was acting on orders. If he hadn't done it, he would have been killed".
>
> "My father lived to a great age. Most of his associates died horrible early deaths. I am eternally grateful he didn't die like that. He chose his own time to go after confessing to his sins."

19

Mickey Spillane
The Last Of The Gentleman Gangsters

WHEN most people hear the name Mickey Spillane, they immediately think of the author famous for his iconic tough no-nonsense detective character, Mike Hammer. Even though he has sold over 225 million books, I don't want to talk about him. The other Mickey Spillane I want to tell you about was no author, but the head of the Irish mob in New York's Hell's Kitchen, Michael (Mickey) Spillane, also known as the last of the gentlemen gangsters.

Mickey Spillane was born to Irish-American parents on July 13, 1933, into the harsh environment of Hell's Kitchen in Manhattan. Also known as Clinton, it is a neighbourhood on the west side of Midtown Manhattan in New York City. It is traditionally considered to be bordered by 34th Street to the south, 59th Street to the north, Eighth Avenue to the east, and the Hudson River to the west.

Hell's Kitchen was a strong hold of the Irish mob in New York and had received its name from 'Dutch Fred', a veteran policeman, who with his rookie partner watching a small riot on West 39th Street near Tenth Avenue. The rookie is supposed to have said, "This place is hell itself", to which Fred replied, "Hell's a mild climate. This is Hell's Kitchen."

Spillane started his crime career early as a young boy, operating as a runner in the illegal gambling numbers racket that was rife and highly profitable in the poorer areas of New York.

The numbers racket was an illegal lottery played mostly, but not exclusively, in the working class neighbourhoods throughout the United States. Started in Harlem, New York, it soon spread to wherever organised crime had a foothold. The premise was simple; for a small bet you picked three digits to match those that will be randomly drawn the following day. In later years, Dutch Shultz would revolutionise the racket to maximise profit for the mob. The "number drawn" would be the last three digits of "the handle", the amount race track bettors placed on a race day at a major racetrack, published in racing journals and major newspapers in New York.

Mickey proved to be a highly reliable numbers runner and was spotted by Eddie McGrath, the Mob boss of Hell's Kitchen and leader of the Longshoreman's union.

McGrath decided to mentor Spillane and marked him out as his successor. Mickey also became a member of The Westies Gang.

The Westies was a predominantly Irish-American organised crime association and a "hit squad" for the Gambino crime family.

The Westies became synonymous with the last generation of Irish in the birthplace of the Irish mob.

Rising in the Irish mob opened up opportunities for

Spillane and he also rose in social circles, marrying Maureen McManus, the daughter of the Democratic district leader, Eugene McManus.

The McManus family had run the Midtown Democratic Club since 1905. This union of political power with criminal activity enhanced Spillane's ability to control union jobs and labour racketeering. This allowed him to move away from the declining waterfront and focus more strongly on construction jobs and service work at the New York Coliseum, Madison Square Garden, and later the Jacob K. Javits Convention Centre.

Mickey and Maureen had three children — Michael (Mickey), Robert and Denise.

Robert would go on to be an actor with roles in *The Thomas Crown Affair* and *NYPD Blue*. He tragically died in 2010, when he fell six storeys to his death when he leaned against his apartment window screen.

Eddie McGrath decided that the ongoing investigation into organised crime on the New York waterfront was becoming too intense and he decided to retire to Florida, handing over his criminal network to his chosen successor, Mickey Spillane, who was now the undisputed leader of the Irish mob and the Westies Gang in Hell's Kitchen.

Whilst organised crime in New York was dominated by the Italian Mafia, they stayed out of the Hell's Kitchen area while Mickey Spillane was the boss.

Spillane was both respected and feared by the Mafia. Often when he needed money he would kidnap members of the Italian Mafia and use the ransom money for his operations.

It was as the boss of the Hell's Kitchen Irish mob he

acquired the label of the 'last of the gentlemen gangsters', a strange epitaph indeed for someone involved in organised crime.

While Spillane was heavily involved in gambling, the numbers racket and loan sharking he never allowed the sale of drugs in his area, a choice which earned him a lot of enemies in the mob but the admiration of the people in Hell's Kitchen. Spillane also sent flowers to neighbours in the hospital and provided turkeys to needy families during Thanksgiving.

His son Robert Spillane remembered the days his father ran the rackets:

"Mickey walked around in $5,000 suits into restaurants where everybody knew him. Heads would turn and people would say things like 'Hey, you know who that is? That's Mickey Spillane!'"

In 1966 Spillane began a long war with his ultimate nemesis, James 'Jimmy C 'Coonan, who was an 18-year-old Irish mobster seeking revenge for the Spillane-initiated kidnapping and pistol whipping of Coonan's father.

Incensed by the treatment meted out to his father, the young Coonan, a notorious hothead, fired an automatic machine gun at Spillane and his associates from atop a Hell's Kitchen tenement building. Although Coonan wounded noone, Spillane understood that the younger hoodlum was not to be taken lightly — and that he would have to be dealt with.

However, that would have to wait as Coonan was imprisoned for a short period of time because of murder and kidnapping charges that were plea-bargained down to a Class C Manslaughter felony charge.

He was released in late 1971 and continued his war

with the Westies and grew his criminal career as part of the Gambino Mafia family who wanted to move in on the Hell's Kitchen area.

Spillane was fiercely independent and his refusal to allow the Italian mobsters to participate in the Hell's Kitchen rackets and his ongoing war with Coonan would lead to his eventual downfall.

Controlling the construction unions was proving highly lucrative. The amount of money Madison Square Garden, the waterfront and unions were generating for Spillane was enormous and when plans were announced for the Jacob K Javits Convention Centre, the Italian Mafia was desperate for what they believed was their piece of the pie.

However, Spillane refused to allow an encroachment on his power base and this led to the New York Irish v Italian mob war.

Although the Italian gangsters greatly outnumbered the members of the Irish mob, Spillane was successful in keeping control of the convention centre and Hell's Kitchen. The Italians, frustrated and embarrassed by their defeat to Spillane and the Irish gangsters, decided to seek revenge.

Hell's Kitchen was no longer safe for Spillane and his family, and he moved to the Irish working-class neighbourhood of Woodside in Queens. With Spillane gone, his control of the rackets in Hell's Kitchen began to deteriorate; Coonan returned and became the neighbourhood's boss.

However, on the New York crime commission, Spillane was still viewed as the Irish mob boss on the Westside, putting the Javits Convention Centre construction site under his control.

Anthony Salerno, a high-ranking member of the Genovese crime family, wanted the centre for himself and reached an agreement with Jimmy Coonan. If Coonan became boss, Salerno would run the construction site and give Coonan a proportion of the proceeds.

Salerno then reached out to Buffalo crime family associate and freelance hitman, Joseph Sullivan, to eliminate the three main Spillane supporters in Hell's Kitchen, Tom Devaney, Tom Kapatos, and Edward Cummiskey.

Cummiskey had apparently switched sides to the Coonan camp, but Salerno and Sullivan were not aware of the switch. Devaney and Cummiskey were murdered in late 1976, and Kapatos was killed in January 1977.

Spillane was now out of the picture, and while Coonan was the undisputed boss of Hell's Kitchen and the Westies, it was felt that Spillane still had to die.

On May 13, 1977, Roy DeMeo, a Gambino crime family soldier, murdered Spillane, aged 43, outside his apartment in Queens as a favour to Coonan.

DeMeo was never charged. Instead a low level mob hitman, Mickey Featherstone, stood trial for the murder and was found not guilty. Nobody has ever been found guilty of the murder of Mickey Spillane.

Thus ended the short but memorable career of Mickey Spillane, the last of the gentlemen gangsters.

Jimmy Coonan was now the boss of the Hell's Kitchen mob and the Westies, but the independence of the Irish gangsters had been lost to the Italian Mafia.

In 1988, Coonan was sentenced to 60 years in prison on assorted charges and is currently serving time in Lewisburg Federal Penitentiary.

20

Henry Hill
The Irish Goodfella

WHEN you think of great gangster films, two names will normally come to mind — *The Godfather* and *Goodfellas*. The former focused on the Sicilian Mafia while the latter on an Irish-American gangster, Henry Hill.

The 1990 movie directed by Martin Scorsese is an adaptation of the 1985 non-fiction book, *Wise Guy*, by Nicholas Pileggi. The movie made over $46 million and received six Academy Award nominations, winning one for Best Supporting Actor for Joe Pesci.

Many film critics rate the film as one of the greatest ever made and in 2000 it was selected by the US library of Congress for Preservation in the National Film Registry because of its historical significance.

Ray Liotta played the central figure of the film, Henry Hill, a man whose life story was so dramatic it could have provided enough material for a whole series of films.

Born on June 11, 1943, Henry Hill was one of nine children born to Henry Hill sr, an Irish immigrant and his Sicilian wife, Carmela Costa Hill, in Manhattan, New

York. The young Henry was raised in Brownsville, a socially deprived area of Brooklyn.

Raised in poverty, Henry was drawn to what he perceived was the glamour of the local mobsters, who were members of the Lucchese crime family. Their base was across the street from the Hill family home. They were led by Paul Vario, a Mafia Capo, who Henry would in future refer to as 'Big Paulie'.

The turning point in Henry's life came when he was just 11 years old in 1955, when he started an after-school job in the Vario mobster-run cab office. In his early teens, he graduated from cleaning up to running errands for the Vario gang.

In 1956 he would meet a man who would be his partner in crime for many years, the notorious hijacker and gambler and Lucchese family associate, James 'Jimmy the Gent' Burke, who was played by Robert De Niro in the movie.

Henry, still only 13, was serving drinks at a card game when he was in awe of Burke's generous tipping.

Hill recalled:

"Twenty here. Twenty there. He wasn't like anyone else I had ever met".

At 14, the Lucchese family arranged for Henry to receive a much sought after union card in the Bricklayers local.

Henry would now be permanently on the payroll of a Mafia-controlled building contractor. However, he would be a 'no show', which meant he was not expected to turn up for work but still guaranteed a very lucrative weekly salary.

A portion of his salary was given as tribute to Big Paulie and Henry was now on the Lucchese family payroll. He dropped out of high school and worked exclusively for the Vario gangsters.

He concentrated on collecting debts and the numbers racket amongst construction workers.

He would soon graduate to more violent mob activity. Still only 15, he was involved in an arson attack on a rival cab company.

The Vario brothers operated a taxi firm as part of their criminal network. The Rebel Cab Company, a legitimate business, opened up just around the corner from the Varios' base. This was unacceptable to Big Paulie, who wanted it put out of business.

Vito 'Tuddy' Vario, Big Paulie's younger brother, took Henry as his accomplice. They drove to the rival cab company with a drum of gasoline in the back seat of their car.

Henry smashed all the cab windows and filled them with newspapers soaked in gasoline. Hill then set them ablaze. And that was the end of the Rebel Cab Company.

Henry's first arrest came when he was 16 and already a Mafia veteran. Hill and Big Paulie's nephew Lenny were caught trying to use a stolen credit card to buy snow tyres.

Despite a tough police interrogation, Henry said nothing but his name and refused to cooperate with the police. The Vario brothers' personal attorney arranged for Henry's release on bail and he was greeted as a hero. He received a suspended sentence and his refusal to talk earned him respect and greatly impressed Jimmy Burke, who saw great potential in the young Hill.

He also saw a kindred spirit. Burke, like Hill, could never be a Mafia 'made man' as he was not 100% Sicilian. However, the Vario crew and the Lucchese family did not discriminate and were happy to have associates of any ethnicity, as long as they made money and did not snitch.

At 17, Henry joined the US army in a move he later described as an attempt to stay out of jail.

He served for three years with the 82nd Airborne Division at Fort Bragg in North Carolina.

Hill was so accustomed to his life of crime that throughout his time in the army, he kept in touch with his mob associates and used his position in charge of the kitchen detail to his advantage. He sold surplus food, acted as a loan shark and sold tax free cigarettes.

Henry also spent two months in the army stockade for stealing a local sheriff's car and then picking a fight with visiting marines.

Discharged in 1963, Henry returned to Big Paulie and a life of crime. He soon began working with Jimmy Burke and hijacking trucks — but bigger things awaited.

Two years later Henry met his future wife Karen Friedman on a double date as the wing man to Paul Vario jnr. *Goodfellas* documents their disastrous date and the fact Henry stood her up on their next date.

However, Karen was seduced by Henry's glamorous lifestyle funded by illegal activity and the two later married in a lavish wedding attended by Hill's mobster friends.

In January 1967, Henry received a tip-off from mob associate, Robert 'Frenchy' Mahon, that the Air France cargo terminal at JFK International airport had stored large amounts of money up to between $400,000 and $700,000 with minimal security.

Henry began to put together a plan and started to investigate the airport closely. He decided that an armed robbery would be unlikely to succeed and was very risky. Instead he began to monitor the security guard who kept the keys to the strong room on him at all times. He learned during his surveillance of the guard on duty that he had a weakness for women.

Hill and Mahon befriended the guard and got him drunk. They then drove him to the Jade East Motel and arranged for a prostitute to entertain the guard. Henry took the distracted guard's keys from his discarded trousers and quickly made a copy and returned the originals.

The guard was none the wiser and did not realise the danger he and his employers were now in.

On April 7, 1967, the newlywed Hill and his associate Tommy DeSimone (later played by Joe Pesci in *Goodfellas*) drove to JFK and entered the Air France cargo terminal. Using the keys they had copied, Henry and DeSimone calmly entered the strong room and loaded $420,000 ($3.1 million in today's terms) into a large suitcase.

Hill and DeSimone confidently walked out of the cargo terminal unchallenged without firing a shot.

The alarm was raised four days later, but by then Henry and his associate had faded into the background.

Henry, as *Goodfellas* shows, did the right thing and shared the money from the robbery with senior Mafia members. He gave $120,000 each to Big Paulie Vario and Sebastian Aloi of the Colombo crime family. He did this because the cargo terminal was located in Colombo territory.

Henry, now a rich young man, used the proceeds from

the heist to buy the 'Suite', a restaurant in Queens. Hill initially thought he could give legitimate business a go. However, within weeks the venue was soon the haunt of his mobster friends and their associates.

In later years, Henry would describe how the club became the venue of choice for members and high ranking leaders of both the Gambino and Lucchese crime families.

The Suite played a prominent part in *Goodfellas*, especially the 1970 murder of William 'Billy Batts' Devino, a Gambino family member and a 'made man'.

Devino had just been released from prison and a welcome home party was held in the Suite. During the party Devino and Tommy DeSimone had an argument. Jimmy Burke and DeSimone started to plan revenge and resolved to murder Devino.

The argument was all a setup. The actual motive for the murder involved loan-sharking rackets which Devino had run before he went to prison.

DeSimone and Burke had taken them over while Devino was in prison, and they did not want to give them up.

Several weeks after the argument, DeSimone and Burke ensured Devino was heavily drunk while in the Suite. DeSimone pistol-whipped Devino unconscious and then, assuming he was dead, they called Hill to drive them to dispose of the body.

Henry had anticipated what was about to happen and had left the Suite, but the phone call dragged him back in as an accomplice. All three drove to Pennsylvania to dispose of the body in the hope it would not be found.

They assumed Devino was dead but during the drive noises were heard coming from the trunk. Hill stopped the car to investigate. Opening the boot, a barely alive Devino cried out for help.

Henry stood back while Burke and DeSimone stabbed Devino to death. Henry would later tell friends that the brutal way in which Devino was murdered haunted his dreams for the rest of his life.

In 1972 Henry's luck finally ran out and he was arrested for extortion. Hill and Burke had severely beaten and pistol-whipped Gaspar Ciacco, a Tampa, Florida gambler who owed union official friends of theirs a large gambling debt. They were found guilty and sentenced to ten years in prison.

Hill was paroled in 1978 after serving five years while Burke was also released on parole around the same time. While in jail, Hill had been involved in supplying drugs to other prisoners.

On his release Big Paulie Vario warned him not to continue with the drug trade. Vario was opposed to the drugs trade for two reasons. Firstly, he did not want drugs in his neighbourhood. Secondly, and more selfishly, he feared that the long sentences imposed for drugs trafficking could encourage members of his crew to become informants in return for a shorter sentence.

Henry was not to be deterred and, seduced by the enormous profits to be made, set about establishing a major drug trafficking operation. He did this in partnership with Paul Mazzei, whom Hill had met in prison. The potential to earn large amounts of money was too great to resist and the money began to roll in.

Mazzei and Hill also set up a gambling racket which was put in place when Mazzei convinced Boston College basketball centre Rick Kuhn to participate. Kuhn encouraged teammates to join the scheme, which would later become a great scandal.

Hill also claimed to have an NBA referee who worked games at Madison Square Garden in his pocket, because of the debts the referee had incurred gambling on horse races.

Burke, the great gambler, wanted in on the action and became partners with Hill and Mazzei in both drug trafficking and the illegal bets.

However, Hill was soon under surveillance by the authorities who began to wiretap his home. Later that year Hill and Burke played major roles in orchestrating the Lufthansa heist.

The Lufthansa heist was a robbery at JFK international Airport on December 11, 1978. This was, at the time the largest robbery ever committed in America. Hill and Burke assembled a gang of 11 mobsters and stole $5,875 million, which is more than $20 million today. This was $5 million in cash and $875,000 in jewellery. The heist is the pivotal part of the *Goodfellas* plot and the sum of money stolen led to one the longest investigations in American criminal history. The last arrest for crime came in 2014.

Jimmy Burke was the mastermind of the crime but he was never formally charged for the crime. Hill's association with the heist would have major ramifications.

Burke, frightened of being informed on, had murdered several of the Lufthansa heist participants. Tommy DeSimone had also disappeared and Henry believed that Big Paulie had participated in his murder along with the Gambino crime family as revenge for the disappearance of 'made man' Billy 'Batts' Devino. These events, combined with Henry's rapidly out of control drug habit, made him increasingly paranoid.

Henry was arrested on April 27, 1980, on a narcotics trafficking charge. Given bail, his freedom was short-lived, as he was quickly re-arrested as a material witness in the Lufthansa heist.

Henry was fearful he would be murdered by his friends — Big Paulie Vario (for disobeying his explicit order not to deal drugs), and Jimmy Burke (to stop him implicating him in the Lufthansa robbery). His fears were confirmed when the FBI and prosecutor Ed McDonald played him back a surveillance tape which was a conversation between Burke and Vario.

Meeting in a roadside café, Burke is heard telling Vario they have to have Henry whacked.

This was confirmed in 2011 when former mobster Greg Bucceroni alleged that he had been approached by Jimmy Burke to murder Hill at a Brooklyn grocery store. Luckily for Hill, Bucceroni declined the contract.

Now convinced he was to be killed, Henry Hill began to talk. One month after his narcotics trafficking arrest on May 27, 1980, Hill decided to become an informant and signed into the US Department of Justice witness protection programme.

Hill was an important coup for the authorities and his testimony led to 50 convictions. Burke and several other Lucchese crime family members were arrested by federal authorities.

Jimmy Burke was given 20 years for the 1978-79 Boston College points shaving scandal involving Boston College basketball games. Burke died of cancer in jail aged 63 on April 13, 1996.

Paul Vario received four years for helping Hill obtain a no-show job to get him paroled from prison. He also received a further 10 years in prison for extortion of air freight companies at JFK Airport. He died in 1988, aged 73, in Fort Worth federal prison.

Hill, his wife Karen, and their two children changed their names, and moved to undisclosed locations in Omaha, Nebraska, then Independence, Kentucky, and eventually Redmond, Washington.

While Hill's life before had been dramatic, his years after becoming an informant were equally colourful.

He was relocated numerous times due to breaches of the witness protection protocols.

In 1987 Hill was arrested in Seattle on narcotics-related charges where he was living in the Wedgewood area under the name of Alex Canclini.

While living in Seattle, Hill was fond of entertaining his neighbours. At one such event, a barbecue, he became intoxicated with a cocktail of drink and drugs and bragged about his true identity to his stunned neighbours.

His federal minders were forced to relocate him to Sarasota in Florida. However, after just a few months, the by now drug-addicted Hill outed himself again.

In 1989, he and his wife Karen divorced after 25 years of marriage. Exasperated by continual security breaches and his continuing criminal activities, the authorities finally snapped and expelled him from the federal witness protection programme in the early 1990s.

After living under aliases such as Martin Lewis and Peter Haines, Hill reassumed his own name. In October 2002, Hill published *The Wise Guy Cookbook: My Favou-*

rite Recipes from My Life as a Goodfella to Cooking on the Run.

In it, Hill shared some stories throughout his childhood, life in the mob, and running from the law. He also presents recipes he learned from his family, during his years in the mob, and some that he came up with himself.

Hill claimed to be clean until he was arrested in North Platte, Nebraska, in March 2005. Hill had left his luggage at Lee Bird Field Airport in North Platte, Nebraska containing drug paraphernalia, glass tubes with cocaine and methamphetamine residue. Hill battled alcoholism for years, claiming at one point that prison had saved his life.

Henry worked for a time as a chef at an Italian restaurant in Nebraska and his spaghetti sauce, Sunday Gravy, was marketed over the internet.

Hill opened a restaurant, Wiseguys, in West Haven, Connecticut, in October 2007.

In 2008 he moved to Malibu with his Italian fiancée, Lisa Caserta. Hill began painting and sold many of his works on eBay.

Now that both Burke and Big Paulie were dead, Henry became more confident and whilst always looking over his shoulder for a Mafia hitman, he and Lisa appeared in several documentaries. Henry also became a regular on *The Howard Stern Show.*

He returned to rehab in 2008, but during that period was arrested twice for public intoxication. Hill was sentenced to two years' probation on March 26, 2009.

On December 14, 2009 he was arrested in Fairview Heights, Illinois, for disorderly conduct and resisting arrest which Hill attributed to his drinking problems.

In reference to his many victims, Hill stated in an interview in March 2008, with BBC's Heather Alexander:

"I don't give a heck what those people think; I'm doing the right thing now."

Henry Hill had a turbulent relationship with his children, Gregg and Gina. They were 13 and 11 when they started a new life in witness protection and experienced a nomadic existence. They would go on to write a book, *On the Run, a Mafia Childhood*, documenting their experiences.

In the book, Gregg told how their father only made things worse for them on the run, constantly resuming his criminal activities, exposing the family while mafia mobsters sought to kill them all.

He also explained how Hill spent his days at the racetrack gambling and his nights drinking.

Hill died on June 12, 2012 in Los Angeles. He had suffered a heart attack before his death and died of complications from long-time heart problems related to smoking.

Hill's family was present when he died and he was cremated the day after his death.

His fiancée Lisa said of his death:

"He went out pretty peacefully, for a Goodfella."

21

James 'Jimmy The Gent' Burke

The Dapper Assassin

IN Martin Scorsese's 1990 film *Goodfellas*, James 'Jimmy the Gent' Burke was played by Robert De Niro. He was portrayed as a dapper, charismatic associate of the New York Mafia. In reality he was a brutal paranoid man responsible for more than 50 murders.

James Burke was born James Conway in New York on July 5, 1931 to Jane Conway, a prostitute who had recently emigrated from her native Dublin. His natural father was never identified. The infant James was soon deposited in a Roman Catholic orphanage, and he would never see his birth mother again.

Raised for many years by nuns and then farmed out to a series of foster homes and orphanages he was subjected to both sexual and psychical abuse — which would have a profound influence and shape his temperament in later years.

Young Conway was fostered in his early teens by a particularly violent man. When he was 13, a bizarre incident led to him being sent back to the abusive Catholic orphanage.

While James was arguing with his foster brothers in the back of the car, his foster father — who had a violent temper — turned around to hit him. He subsequently lost control of the car and ran into oncoming traffic. He died in the crash.

James, who was unscathed, was never forgiven by his foster mother, who administered regular beatings until she sent him back to the nuns.

At the age of 14, James Conway was adopted by the Burke family, who lived in a large wooden boarding house on Rockaway Beach Boulevard, in the New York suburb of Queens.

This proved to be a happy home and he remained close to the Burke family and visited his adoptive mother and father without fail every Mother's Day, Christmas and on their birthdays.

Later in life when he was making large amounts as a criminal he would send them money every month in an unmarked envelope. This was usually several thousand dollars.

The young James, whilst disturbed and traumatised by his brutal experiences in the Roman Catholic orphanage system and various foster homes, had at last found loving parents and peace and calm. However, the damage to his personality had been done and he soon turned to crime.

Despite his later success, his early attempts at crime did not bode well and between the ages of 16 and 22, he enjoyed just 86 days outside of prison.

Aged 17 Burke met and was mentored by Dominick 'Remo' Cersani, an Italian-American gangster who served as a 'Caporegime' in the Colombo crime family.

He was soon a key ally of Cersani and became a silent partner with him in garment factories in Queens and despite being too young to drink, a bar, the Robert's Lounge, also in Queens.

In September 1949, the 18-year-old Burke was arrested for trying to pass on $3,000 worth of fraudulent cheques for Cersani.

He was found guilty and sentenced to five years in Auburn correctional facility for bank forgery after refusing to implicate Cersani. His staunch refusal to succumb to police pressure and inform on his mentor would stand him in good stead. Whilst his Irish background meant he could never be a mafia 'made man', his silence ensured he was soon accepted into the Mafia criminal world. An impressed Cersani dubbed him 'The Irish Guinea', and arranged for associates in the prison to protect him.

In prison, he mixed with a number of mafia members and other criminals of all nationalities in the New York area. He also became close to members of both the Lucchese and Colombo crime families who would feature prominently in his later life of crime.

On his release he used his connections with the Lucchese crime family, who controlled the construction rackets in New York to begin a trade as a bricklayer.

He soon tired of an honest life and decided to return to a life of crime using the reputation and connections he had made in prison.

During the 1950s, in addition to other crimes, he was involved in other illegal activity such as distributing untaxed cigarettes and liquor.

In the 60s, working again with Dominick Cersani,

he was involved in loan sharking, cigarette smuggling, armed robbery and hijacking.

In 1962 Jimmy married his wife Michelle 'Mickey' Burke. Just before the wedding he found out his future wife's ex-fiancé was still in contact with his bride-to-be. On the day of the wedding, the unfortunate man was found dead, his body chopped up in his car.

The couple would go on to have four children — two daughters, Catherine and Phoebe, and two sons, who Jimmy sardonically called Frank and Jesse in homage to fellow criminals.

Given his sad childhood it's ironic that he would go on to neglect his son Jesse so badly due to his stutter, which Jimmy saw as a sign of weakness. Jesse would not be involved in a life of crime.

Frank would go on to be a drug addict and petty criminal. Frank James Burke was found by police, shot to death on 1043 Liberty Avenue in the Cypress Hills section of Brooklyn, New York, at 2.30am on May 18, 1987. He was 27 years old. There is no record of any remorse or grief from Jimmy Burke about the death of his son.

Jimmy's daughter Catherine married into a crime family and she and her husband still live in the Burke family home in Queens.

Jimmy ran his operations out of the Robert's Lounge in Queens. This was a favourite haunt of the underworld and frequented by members of both the Lucchese and Colombo crews. James ran a loan shark and bookmaking operation that was based at the bar, and high stakes poker games in the basement, from which he would receive a share.

Burke also owned a dress factory, Moo Moo Vedda's, which kept him well supplied with laundered money.

Burke would become mentor to three members of the Lucchese crime family — Angelo Sepe, Thomas DeSimone and Henry Hill. They started small, moving on stolen goods but eventually graduated to being part of Burke's criminal crew and helped Jimmy with the hijacking of trucks around the New York airports.

Jimmy was now building a reputation as a good earner, using charm and menace.

Burke was already an immense figure, standing at 6'2" and his time as a bricklayer had given him a muscular frame which, combined with his broken nose and fiery temper, made him a man not to cross.

Henry Hill would later tell FBI agents of how everyone feared Burke. He described Jimmy thus:

"He was a big guy and knew how to handle himself. He looked like a fighter. He had a broken nose and he had a lot of hands. If there was just the littlest amount of trouble, he'd be all over you in a second. He'd grab a guy's tie and slam his chin into the table before the guy knew he was in a war... Jimmy had a reputation for being wild. He'd whack you."

However, it was the hijacking operation that would give Jimmy his lifelong nickname, 'The Gent'.

Whilst he used violence whenever he felt it was necessary and never shirked from brutal murders, Jimmy would treat the drivers of lorries that he hijacked well and even tip them to keep their mouth shut. Henry Hill in his memoirs recalled how Burke would usually give $50 to the drivers of the trucks they stole, as if he were tipping them for the inconvenience, which led to his nickname 'Jimmy the Gent'. But a gent with a temper.

When Jimmy was informed about a young associate who had refused to pay back a $5,000 loan from his elderly mother, he paid the woman out of his own pocket — and then had the son killed.

Jimmy even ordered the murder of his best friend, mentor and co-owner of the Robert's Lounge, Dominick 'Remo' Cersani.

Cersani became a police informant and helped the authorities arrest Burke on a charge of truck hijacking. While Jimmy managed to beat the rap, he had his friend murdered and buried next to the bocce court behind his bar, the Robert's Lounge.

Associates would later describe that whenever Jimmy played bocce with his friends, he would jokingly say:

"Hey Remo, how're you doing?"

Jimmy had a novel way of getting people to pay back their debts. When Burke had a problem collecting money he was owed, and the unfortunate debtor had children, he would pick the child up in his huge arm, open the refrigerator with the other, and say:

"If you don't do whatcha supposed to, I'm gonna lock your kid inside the fuckin' refrigerator."

Everyone paid up.

The money was now flowing into Jimmy's coffers. He and his gangster crew plundered Kennedy Airport at will. Using the Luccheses' control over the unions, Jimmy and his crew made massive amounts of money from a variety of criminal activities especially hijacking. Their success was built on a mixture of bribery and violence and they operated at impunity, murdering anyone who would provide information on them to the police.

Jimmy would ensure that the authorities were well bribed and law enforcement officers would tell Burke and his crew of any potential witnesses or informants. These unfortunate people would soon find themselves dead and unable to harm Burke and his operation.

Every year as many as 12 bodies — tied up, strangled, and shot — a year would be found in the trunks of stolen vehicles and abandoned in the parking lots surrounding JFK Airport.

Henry Hill also said about Burke:

"Jimmy could plant you just as fast as shake your hand. It didn't matter to him. At dinner he could be the nicest guy in the world, but then he could blow you away for dessert."

The good times came to an end when Jimmy and Henry Hill were doing a favour for Lucchese crime boss, Paul 'Big Paulie' Vario.

In 1972 they were both arrested for badly beating fellow mobster Gaspar Ciaccio in Tampa, Florida.

They had been sent by Vario to ensure Ciaccio repaid a gambling debt to their mutual friend and union boss, Casey Rosado.

Charged with extortion, Jimmy and Hill were found guilty and sentenced to ten years in federal prison.

They both served five years and were then paroled. Henry Hill had started dealing drugs in prison and on his release, set up a lucrative drug trafficking operation. Burke, seeing the vast profits being made, wanted in.

He and Hill became partners, but kept this secret from the Lucchese crime family, who forbade its members from being involved in the drug trade — not out of any moral compass, but to selfishly ensure that none of its members would be caught and become informants, under the threat of hefty prison sentences. Ironically, this is what Hill would eventually do.

The pinnacle of Burke's criminal career and which would eventually lead to his downfall was the 1978 Lufthansa Heist, the robbery of nearly $6 million in cash and jewels from Building 261 at the Lufthansa cargo terminal at John F. Kennedy International Airport. This was the largest robbery in American history at the time.

The idea for the robbery came from inside information provided to Burke and Hill from a Lufthansa cargo supervisor, Louis Werner, who owned a large gambling debt to a Burke-controlled bookie, Martin Krugman.

Unable to pay his debt and aware of Burke's method of dealing with defaulters, Werner attempted to write off his debt and save his life by providing Burke and Hill with an opportunity they could not resist. This was the opportunity to rob the loosely guarded Lufthansa cargo terminal where large amounts of cash were transferred to pay American GIs in Germany.

Because JFK Airport was divided between the Gambino crime family and the Lucchese family, permission was needed to go ahead. Lucchese capo Big Pauli Vario was a close friend of Burke and Hill, so that was not an issue. However, permission was asked and granted by the Gambino capo who controlled the airport. This was given be a certain John Gotti.

In the book *Wiseguys* by Henry Hill and Nicholas Pileggi, they detailed how Gotti met with both Burke and Hill at a restaurant in Queens and discussed the robbery beforehand, with Gotti agreeing to provide assistance.

According to Hill, it was agreed that Gotti would supply a warehouse where the crew could transfer the loot from the getaway van to a switch car to help evade cops. Gotti would then handle the destruction of the getaway van at a mob-controlled salvage yard after the heist was completed.

For his cooperation and help in the scheme, Gotti wanted $250,000 and a Gotti associate, Paolo LiCastri, was to be an added part of the crew, to ensure the Gambinos' interests were looked after.

With the green light Burke set about formulating a plan and assembling an 11-man crew to carry out the robbery.

This included Angelo Sepe, Tommy DeSimone, Louis 'The Whale' Cafora, Joseph 'Joe Buddha' Marni, Robert 'Frenchy' McMahon and the Gambino gunman, Paolo LiCastri.

Jimmy's son Frank was recruited to drive a 'crash car'. This was a car used to ram any police cars in pursuit of the getaway vehicles.

Parnell 'Stacks' Edwards, an African-American mobster, was taken on board, not to be part of the robbery crew, but to dispose of the security van used in the robbery at a junk yard compactor in New Jersey.

Using the inside information provided by the Lufthansa employee Louise Werner, Burke and his crew carried out the robbery early on the morning of December 11, 1978.

At 3am a van containing five robbers wearing dark clothing and ski masks arrived at the Lufthansa cargo terminal. A crash car driven by Frank Burke waited in the parking lot. Three men got out of the van and entered the front door of the cargo terminal. The two men left in the van drove to the rear of the building. They then cut the lock on the security fence and replaced it with one of their own.

The three armed robbers who had entered the building had been informed 3am was 'lunch hour' for the shift, and most personnel were already in the cafeteria which made it easier to round them all up. When the two robbers in the van returned to the front of the building, they encountered a security guard who was pistol whipped and handcuffed. One of the robbers led the security guard inside the building, where he was forced to the floor.

At gunpoint the shift supervisor was forced to deactivate the general alarm system as well as all additional silent alarms within the vault, and escort the robbers inside. The supervisor was forced to open the cargo bay door.

The robbers then drove the van inside the loading bay and packed it with every bag of untraceable currency and jewellery they found in the vault.

After the van was loaded, the supervisor was taken back to the lunchroom, handcuffed, and forced to the floor next to the other employees. The robbers ordered the employees not to make a move for at least 15 minutes. To ensure compliance, the robbers confiscated the wallets of every employee and threatened the lives of their families if instructions were not followed.

This 15-minute buffer was crucial because Werner's inside information made the robbers aware that the Port Authority Police could seal off the entire airport within 90 seconds, preventing any vehicle or person from coming in or going out.

At 4.21am, the van containing the robbers and the stolen cash pulled out of the cargo terminal and left JFK, followed by the crash car, and drove to a garage in Canarsie, Brooklyn, where Jimmy Burke was waiting. There, the money was switched to a third vehicle that was driven away by Jimmy Burke and his son Frank.

The rest of the robbers left and drove home, except the Gambino gun man, Paolo LiCastri, who insisted on taking the subway home.

The only flaw in the plan was that Parnell Edwards, who was supposed to put stolen license plates on the van used in the robbery and then dispose of it, did not take it to be compacted for scrap. Instead he got high, passing out at a girlfriend's house, leaving the truck outside in a no parking zone. The next day the van was discovered by police with his fingerprints all over it.

Jimmy and his son Frank drove the stolen sacks to a safe house to be counted. It was during this count that the true magnitude of the robbery hit Jimmy.

He had anticipated a haul of around $2-3 million. Instead the final count was $5 million in cash and $875,000 in jewellery, making it the largest cash robbery committed on American soil at the time.

Burke's take of the haul was a little over $2.4m. Lucchese Capo Big Paulie Vario received $1m and John Gotti received the $250,000 he had agreed upon. The rest was split amongst the robbers and the support crew. Very few received more than $50k and many would not live to spend it.

The size of the Lufthansa haul shocked Jimmy. He knew now that the authorities would be determined to bring his crew to justice.

Regardless of his system of bribes, the publicity generated because of the size of the robbery would mean the local, state and federal authorities would all be involved in a crackdown on organised crime to find the culprits.

When he found out that Parnell Edwards had allowed the robbery van to be found with his fingerprints on it, his paranoia began to increase.

The FBI quickly linked Edwards with Burke and the Lucchese family. They began to bug the phones at the Robert's Lounge and vans belonging to Paulie Vario's crew. While nothing linking Burke to the crime was found, the FBI began to bring in members of Vario's crew for questioning.

An increasingly paranoid Burke decided that people now had to die to ensure he did not go to jail.

The first was Parnell Edwards, who was found shot to death in his apartment in South Ozone Park, Queens on December 18, 1978, one week after the robbery.

Martin Krugman, the bookmaker who provided the tip to Henry Hill and Burke's Robert's Lounge crew, vanished on January 6, 1979. Henry Hill stated that Krugman was killed on the orders of Burke, who did not want to pay Krugman his $500,000 share of the stolen money. Said Hill, in *Wiseguys*:

> "It was a matter of half a million bucks. No way Jimmy was going to deny himself half a million dollars because of Marty Krugman. If Jimmy killed Marty, Jimmy would get Marty's half a mill."

Burke discovered that Theresa Ferrara, a mistress of both Tommy De Simone and Paulie Vario, was brought in by the FBI. This was part of the bugging operation. She was released but Jimmy believed she would crack and turn informant and that sealed her fate. She was murdered on February 10, 1979. Her dismembered torso was found floating in the waters off Barnegat Inlet near Toms River, New Jersey, on May 18, 1979.

Next was Louis Cafora, known as Fat Louis, and his newlywed wife Joanna who were reported missing in March 1979 by her parents. They were never seen again. It was alleged that Cafora agreed to become a police informant and either Burke or Angelo Sepe murdered them and disposed of the bodies.

Thomas Monteleone, an Italian-Canadian mobster, used $250,000 of Lufthansa heist money to become involved in a drug deal with Burke and Richard Eaton (a noted hustler and con-man). The drug deal didn't work out as planned. Monteleone was found dead in Connecticut in March 1979. Not directly related to the Lufthansa Heist, Monteleone's murder appears to have been collateral damage.

Then it was the turn of Robert McMahon and his close friend Joe Manri who were found shot dead in a Buick Electra parked on a Brooklyn street on May 16, 1979.

Even Paolo LiCastri, the Gambino soldier, did not escape. Gotti agreed to his demise and he was found shot to death, his half-naked body smouldering in a garbage-strewn lot in Brooklyn on June 13, 1979.

The only members of the gang to survive the initial carnage were Burke's son, Frank James Burke, Thomas DeSimone, Angelo Sepe and Henry Hill.

Frank James Burke would be shot in a botched drug deal in May 1987. Tommy DeSimone was murdered in 1979 as a reprisal for having killed two of John Gotti's close friends, William 'Billy Batts' Bentvena and Foxy Jerothe.

Angelo Sepe was murdered in 1984, shot in the head when he answered the door one morning at his Brooklyn apartment. This was in retaliation for having robbed a mafia-connected drug dealer.

Increasingly paranoid, Burke allegedly attempted to kidnap and possibly hold to ransom or kill Henry Hill's wife, Karen, and their two children, when he suspected Henry of being an informant.

This was not an unfounded fear, as when Henry Hill was arrested for drug trafficking in 1980, again as a result of the FBI bugging operation following the Lufthansa heist, he did indeed become an FBI informant. He did this to avoid a lengthy prison sentence and he and his family duly entered the Federal Witness Protection Scheme.

Later in 1980, Louis Werner, the Lufthansa employee who had supplied the inside information for the heist and the only person to be actually prosecuted for the robbery, became an informant one year into a 15-year sentence. He did so in hope of an early release.

A search warrant was now issued for Jimmy's bar, Robert's Lounge. Tipped off by a police officer on his payroll, Burke quickly removed the bodies buried on the premise and nearby. These were Dominick 'Remo' Cersani (under the bocce court), and Michael 'Spider' Gianco — a Robert's Lounge bartender who was shot to death by Tommy DeSimone for an insult (previously buried under the basement floor).

Burke was arrested on April 1, 1980 for a parole violation which was associating with a known felon.

In 1982, he was convicted of fixing Boston College basketball games as part of a point-shaving gambling scam in 1978, and was sentenced to 20 years in prison. Burke protested:

"I gave the little bastard (Hill) some bucks to bet on games, that's all!"

The authorities knew he had planned and organised the Lufthansa Heist, but they did not have enough evidence to prove it in a court of law.

Although Burke was suspected of committing more than 50 murders, he was only convicted of one, the murder of Richard Eaton, a hustler and confidence man.

Burke was charged with the murder of Eaton, based on evidence Henry Hill gave to authorities.

At the trial, Hill took the stand and testified against his former friend. Hill said Eaton had convinced Burke to invest $250,000 in a cocaine deal that promised immense profit. Eaton, however, kept the money for his own use.

When at one point Hill asked Burke about Eaton's whereabouts, observing that he hadn't been around in a while, Hill said Burke replied:

"Don't worry about him. I whacked the fucking swindler out."

Burke also told Hill that this would be a lesson to two other drug purchasers who had not yet paid him. Based on the evidence of Burke's name, address, and phone number found in Eaton's coat lining when his body was found and Hill's testimony, Burke was convicted, and on February 19, 1985, he was given a life sentence, protesting "the bastard died of hypothermia!"

When he was leaving New York on an airplane, he looked down at JFK airport and said to an officer:

"Once upon a time that was all mine."

Burke was serving his time in Wende Correctional Facility in Alden, New York, when he developed lung cancer. He died from this disease on April 13, 1996, aged 64, while being treated at Roswell Park Cancer Institute in Buffalo, New York.

Had he lived he would have been eligible for parole in 2004, aged 73.

22

Whitey Bulger
The FBI's $2m Man

IF you have heard of Whitey Bulger, it's probably because of two iconic images. The first is of Johnny Depp in the 2015 film *Black Mass* and the second, the police mugshot of the 82-year-old, grey-haired fugitive who looked like a kindly grandfather captured in 2011, after 16 years on the run.

However, Whitey Bulger was no kindly grandfather. He was one of the FBI's most wanted criminals with a reward of $2m dollars on his head.

James Joseph Bulger was born in Dorchester, Massachusetts, on September 3, 1929 to Irish-American parents, James Joseph senior and Jean Bulger. Bulger was raised in poverty after his father, a longshoreman, lost an arm in an industrial accident.

James and Jean would go on to have six children. Bulger has two younger brothers, William 'Billy' Michael Bulger (born 1934) and John P. Bulger (born 1938).

When James junior was eight, the family moved to the newly built Mary Ellen McCormack housing project in south Boston. The other Bulger children excelled at school, especially William 'Billy' Bulger, who would go on to have a long political career as a Democratic state senator and president of the Massachusetts Senate.

In contrast James junior was drawn into minor crime and had very little schooling. He was described as a child out of control and he even fulfilled his childhood fantasy of running away with a travelling circus, when he was 10 years old. He was quickly reunited with his family.

Young James Bulger first came to the attention of the authorities when he was arrested for stealing at the age of 14. This was just the start of a long criminal career.

In his teens, local police gave Bulger the nickname 'Whitey' because of his blond hair. Bulger hated the name, he preferred to be called 'Jim', 'Jimmy', or even 'Boots'.

The last nickname came from his habit of wearing cowboy boots and his fondness for hiding a switchblade in the boots. However, the nickname 'Whitey' stuck.

In the next few years he joined a street gang known as the 'Shamrocks' and he was arrested for larceny, forgery, assault and battery, and armed robbery. For the last crime he served five years in a juvenile reformatory.

When he was released, Whitey was advised by his family to join the Air Force in an effort to get his life back on track.

After his basic training, he was stationed as an aircraft mechanic, first at the Smoky Hill Air Force Base in Salina, Kansas, then in Idaho. He spent time in the stockade for several assaults. He was later arrested by Air Force police in 1950 for going absent without leave. Surprisingly, he received an honourable discharge in 1952 and returned to Boston.

In 1956, Bulger served his first term in federal prison

when he was sentenced to time in Atlanta penitentiary for armed robbery and truck hijacking.

He later told his close associate and fellow mobster Kevin Weeks, that while in prison, he was involved in the MK-ULTRA programme, the goal of which was to research mind control drugs for the CIA.

For 18 months, Bulger and 18 other inmates, all of whom had volunteered in return for reduced sentences, were given LSD and other drugs. Bulger later complained that they had been "recruited by deception" and were told they were helping to find "a cure for schizophrenia". He described his experience as "nightmarish" and said it took him "to the depths of insanity".

Fearing an escape attempt, the authorities transferred Bulger to Alcatraz for three years and then onto Leavenworth Penitentiary. After nine years' imprisonment, Whitey was paroled. He would never be arrested again or spend a day in jail until his capture in 2011.

A free man, Bulger returned to his roots in south Boston and to his life of crime. He became a loan shark and then an enforcer for the local crime boss, Donald Killeen. After Killeen was gunned down in 1972, Bulger joined The Winter Hill Gang, where he quickly rose up the ranks.

A shrewd, ruthless, cunning mobster, Bulger sanctioned numerous killings, including the murders of Spike O'Toole, Paulie McGonagle, Eddie Connors, Tommy King and Buddy Leonard.

By 1979, Whitey Bulger had become a major player in Boston's organised crime scene. That year, Howie Winter, the boss of The Winter Hill Gang, was sent to prison for fixing horse races, and Bulger assumed the gang's leadership. Over the next 16 years, he came to control a significant portion of Boston's drug dealing, bookmaking and loansharking operations.

During this same time (from 1975 to 1990), unknown to even his closest associates, Bulger was amazingly an FBI informant.

Taking advantage of his brother William's stature in the Massachusetts State Senate and childhood friendships that linked him to members of the police force, Bulger helped bring down the 'Patriarcas', a New England Italian organised crime family. In return, the FBI allowed him to grow his own crime operation unhindered.

Interestingly, one organisation Bulger refused to inform on was the IRA, with whom he enjoyed a close relationship.

Whitey Bulger always thought of himself as an Irish patriot and he and his gang were soon involved in helping the IRA mount an offensive in Northern Ireland.

While enforcing a murderous protection racket around the city's south side, Bulger's Irish-American mob were also running guns to what Bulger called 'the boys back home'.

Patrick Nee, an IRA sympathiser and lieutenant of Bulger described how they started:

"The coffins carrying departed members of Boston's Irish-American clan back across the Atlantic for burial in the land of their fathers were unusually heavy. But no one suspected a thing. We were able to get at least five rifles, a couple of handguns, and some ammunition under a corpse. Caskets were ideal for smuggling."

It was his support for the Irish republican campaign

against Margaret Thatcher's government more than 3,000 miles away that led directly to one of the most gruesome killings of his career after the gang organised one of the biggest weapons shipments to the IRA.

Patrick Nee, who moved to Boston as a boy from a Gaelic-speaking village in County Galway, recalled in his book, 'Criminal and an Irishman, The Inside Story of the Boston Mob and the IRA':

"I think he liked the legitimacy a political cause gave him."

He went on to say:

"Whitey loved being associated with the IRA and the cause of Irish freedom. Living on streets dotted with IRA murals and drinking in pubs where hats were passed round to raise money for the families of IRA prisoners, Bulger's enforcers saw themselves as freedom fighters as much as gangsters.

"Bulger thought he was a criminal with a passion: to drive the British out of Ireland."

Early on, thousands of dollars taken during the gang's shakedowns of bookmakers were funnelled to Ireland through the local representative of Noraid, the Irish republican charity in the US.

However, Bulger was urged to think bigger by Joe Cahill, one of the Provisional IRA's founders, during a meeting at The Three Os, the gang's favourite pub, nicknamed 'The Bucket of Blood'.

Cahill, banned from the US over a conviction for murdering a policeman in Belfast in the 1940s, was sneaked into Boston on a coach full of fans returning from an ice hockey match in Canada.

"Lads," Cahill told them, after showing them a propaganda video of British troops and RUC officers firing rubber bullets at crowds, "we need your help."

Soon Bulger and his gang were shipping 30 rifles, 25 pistols, 10 blocks of C-4 plastic explosive and 2,500 rounds of ammunition to Ireland under the false floor of a Dodge van.

The mission's success thrilled the gang and made them more ambitious.

In 1983 Bulger, Nee and others met John Crawley, a 26-year-old IRA man who had returned to Ireland after serving in an elite unit of the US Marines. They hatched a plan to buy a boat, fill it with weapons and sail it all the way to Ireland.

Over the following months they assembled a seven-ton arsenal after extorting the money from drug-dealers.

The hoard comprised 163 assault rifles, 71,000 rounds of ammunition, a ton of military explosives, and a dozen bulletproof vests. To the astonishment of IRA commanders struggling to obtain weapons at home, they bought much of it from advertisements in the pages of *Shotgun News*.

Other items were obtained from IRA sympathisers around the US — twenty-five mini machine-guns from a gang in Philadelphia; a dozen shotguns from a contact in New York. They were all transferred to bags treated to protect them from the Irish peat bogs in which they were to be buried.

One September night in 1984, the shipment was loaded on to a fishing boat the gang had bought and renamed 'Valhalla', after the heavenly destination for martyrs of combat in Norse mythology.

The core gang had been joined by a handful of new-comers, including John McIntyre, a 31-year-old marine mechanic and drug smuggler. His loose tongue after a few drinks worried the older mobsters, but they accepted that given his seafaring expertise, "he was the guy with balls enough to cross the Atlantic".

Six vans delivered the weapons to the dock in Gloucester, 35 miles north-east of Boston. Finally, three minutes after midnight, the crew set sail.

Following a terrible journey, the weapons were transferred to an Irish boat, which was intercepted by Irish authorities after a tip-off from a British mole inside the IRA. The Valhalla got away and back to Boston. But the very next day, the gang's problems began.

McIntyre was caught trying to enter his estranged wife's house. When police logged his details, an outstanding drink-driving charge showed up. Near breaking point after his harrowing six-week boat trip, and facing a weekend in the cells, he started to talk. "I'd like to get out of here," he pleaded. "And I'd just like to start living a normal life." Soon he was telling police the story of the Valhalla.

Unfortunately for him, as word of his disclosures spread through US agencies, it reached John Connolly, an FBI man who was running Bulger as an informant against rival gangsters. He promptly tipped off the mob boss.

McIntyre was lured to Nee's brother's house on the pretext of delivering beer to a party. Dragged to the basement, he was chained to a chair by Bulger, who demanded to know what he had disclosed, while a rope was tightened around his neck.

Eventually the torture from Bulger, who was waving his MAC-10 machine pistol, became too much, according to another mobster, Kevin Weeks. "Jim says to him, 'do you want one in the head?'," he recalled. "And he says, 'yes, please'."

After Bulger obliged, McIntyre's teeth were extracted with pliers to prevent identification.

Bulger "had to go upstairs and lie down" after "the release of excitement from the killing exhausted him."

Bulger dug a five-foot hole in the ground and buried the body, which was found 16 years later.

Nee, who was jailed for his part in the Valhalla mission, still lives in South Boston.

He denies persistent rumours that he too is a protected FBI mole.

The Winter Hill Gang and Bulger carried on and one highly lucrative money-making scheme was extortion. Bulger would summon local drug dealers to his south Boston headquarters and explain a price was on their head.

He could ensure their safety for a similar sum. Not surprisingly, the money began to flow in for Bulger and his gang.

The FBI has estimated that over the course of his career, Whitey Bulger amassed a personal fortune of over $25 million.

Despite making money from drug dealers, one thing Whitey would not allow in south Boston was heroin. Bulger also strictly forbade the selling of any drugs to children. Any dealer who refused to abide by his gang's rules soon found themselves violently driven out of his turf or worse dead.

In the summer of 1991 Bulger and Kevin Weeks, along

with associates Patrick and Michael Linskey, came into possession of the winning Massachusetts Lottery ticket, which had been bought at a store he owned. The four men shared a prize of around $14 million. Bulger was widely thought to have obtained his share of the jackpot illegitimately.

In the spring of 1994, the Drug Enforcement Administration (DEA), the Massachusetts State Police and the Boston Police Department launched an investigation into Bulger's gambling operations. In early 1995, Bulger and his associate, Stephen Flemmi, were indicted. Bulger, however, managed to evade capture.

According to the authorities, Bulger's FBI handler and longtime friend, Special Agent John Connolly, tipped Bulger off to the 1995 indictment, allowing Whitey to escape with his then girlfriend, Theresa Stanley.

Bulger returned a month later, after Stanley decided that she wanted to return to her children, but he fled again soon after with another mistress, Catherine Greig.

In 1999, Bulger was officially named on the FBI's 'Ten Most Wanted Fugitives' list, at one point being designated the bureau's second most-wanted man, behind only Osama Bin Laden. A $2 million reward was issued for providing any information leading directly to his arrest.

Bulger's life on the run ended in June 2011, when he was caught and arrested in Santa Monica, California, after a 16-year manhunt. A tipster had notified the FBI that the 81-year-old fugitive and Greig had been living in a retirement complex.

It later transpired that the FBI received a tip from a woman in Iceland that Bulger was living in an apartment near a beach in Santa Monica. The *Boston Globe* identified the tipster as Anna Björnsdóttir, a former model, actress, and Miss Iceland 1974, who lived in Bulger's neighbourhood and was rumoured to have been a spurned lover of Bulger's.

The FBI had the building manager lure Bulger to the garage of the apartment by telling him the lock on his storage locker was broken. In the garage, Bulger was surrounded by FBI agents and local police officers. He initially insisted he was his alias, Charlie Gasko, according to FBI special agent Scott Garriola, until he eventually admitted:

"You know who I am; I'm Whitey Bulger."

Inside the apartment, the FBI found 30 guns, more than $822,000 in cash, knives and ammunition, much of which was hidden in the walls. Greig was also captured and, in March 2012, she pleaded guilty to conspiracy to harbouring a fugitive and conspiracy to commit identity fraud. In June 2012, she was sentenced to eight years in prison.

Bulger was brought back to Boston for interrogation about his years on the run. He stunned police officers by detailing a life of travel and luxury. He regularly crossed the US border unhindered into Mexico to buy his heart medication. Ever the canny kid from South Boston, despite his wealth he wanted a bargain.

One bizarre excursion was a visit to his old prison Alcatraz as a tourist. He saw his old cell and even had a photograph taken wearing a striped prison suit and standing behind mock prison bars. Not bad for a man who was second only to Osama Bin Laden on the FBI's most wanted list.

When he arrived in Boston a wave of panic crashed through the local law enforcement as some feared and even anticipated that Bulger, a long-time FBI informant, would reveal the extent of his network of police contacts. Would he reveal those who he had bribed, allowing him to operate his criminal network unhindered for so long?

On July 6, 2011 Whitey Bulger, after 16 years on the run, was finally arraigned in a federal court. He pleaded not guilty to 48 charges, including 19 counts of murder, money laundering, perjury, extortion, obstruction of justice, narcotics distribution and weapons violations.

The authorities took nearly two years to bring Bulger to trial and on June 12, 2013, Bulger went on trial in South Boston's John Joseph Moakley United States Courthouse before Judge Denise J. Casper, on 32 counts of racketeering and firearms possession.

On August 12, 2013, after a two-month trial, a jury began its deliberation for five days and found Bulger guilty on 31 counts, including federal racketeering, extortion, conspiracy and 11 of 19 murders. They found he was not guilty of seven murders and could not reach a verdict on one murder.

Bulger was sentenced to two life sentences, plus five years in prison on November 13, 2013.

According to the *Chicago Tribune*, the sentencing judge, US District Judge Denise Casper told Bulger that:

"The scope, the callousness, the depravity of your crimes are almost unfathomable."

In September 2014, Bulger entered the Coleman II United States Penitentiary in Sumterville, Florida. His register number was 02182-748.

The FBI had finally got their most wanted $2m man.

Bulger was not to die naturally in prison.

As an FBI informant and the man who had helped bring down the Italian mafia in Boston, he was always a marked man.

He was transferred to US Penitentiary Hazelton on Monday, October 29, 2018, one of the most notorious and dangerous prisons in the US penal system.

Questions have been asked why a wheelchair-bound 88-year-old Bulger was transferred to a prison which contained numerous enemies from his time in organised crime, including many mafia soldiers he had helped put behind bars. However, no answers have been given.

At the time of his transfer the press suggested that whoever authorised the move was effectively throwing Bulger into the lion's den.

Bulger had been an inmate at Coleman penitentiary in Florida for four years. On his transfer, Joe Rojas, the union president for correctional staff at the prison, said:

'Sending him there is like a death sentence. It's like going on death row."

Bulger was a hated man at Hazelton and retribution would not be long in being administered.

Just 12 hours after his transfer on Tuesday, October 30, Bulger was attacked by Fotios 'Freddy' Geas and beaten viciously with a lock in a sock.

A lock in a sock is a particularly vicious home-made weapon behind bars. It involves a lock placed in a sock and swung like a mace.

Not only did Geas attack Bulger with the home-made weapon, he also used a shiv to gouge out Bulger's eyes.

Bulger, who was found unresponsive at 8.20am on Tuesday, didn't respond to life-saving measures and was pronounced dead by the Preston County medical examiner.

The 51-year-old Freddy Geas was serving a life sentence for the brutal murders of Gary Westerman and Adolfo 'Big Al' Bruno.

Those who knew Geas described him as a feared killer around his hometown of Western Springfield, Massachusetts, who was prone to outbursts of violence and operated alongside his younger brother, Ty.

While of Greek origin, Geas was a renowned hitman for the Boston mafia, an organisation Bulger had done so much to damage during his years as an FBI informant.

It was later found that Geas sought revenge as he believed Bulger had helped frame one of his friends for murder.

Whitey's brutal death, at the age of 88, was welcomed by the families of many of his victims back in his home turf of Boston.

One of them was Michael Donahue, who in 1982 was driving his neighbour (who ironically happened to be an FBI informant) in a car that was sprayed with gunfire.

Michael's son, Tommy, told CBS's Boston station, WBZ:

> "Bulger spent many years destroying my family, and a lot of other families, so a guy like him doesn't deserve a nice, easy death; he deserves a slow death, and that what I hope he got."

Michael's widow, Patricia, told WBZ:

> "I'm gonna buy myself a bottle of Champagne and I'm going to pop that cork."

"Some people think he had it coming?" a reporter asked.

I leave the final words to her reply:

"He did have it coming, I agree."

Perhaps a fitting epitaph for not only Whitey Bulger, but all the *Irish Wise Guys*.